Sunset

Lawns

The contents of this book are also published as part of the Sunset book
LAWNS & GROUND COVERS

By the Editors of Sunset Books and Sunset Magazine

Grass lushly carpets formal garden, shaded by towering trees.

Sunset Publishing Corporation ■ **Menlo Park, California**

Landscaping with Grass

It's hard to imagine a landscape that doesn't include a lawn. Whether designed as a children's play area, as an adjunct to an entertainment patio, or as a private glen surrounded by trees and other plantings, a lawn provides a lush and inviting surface for many uses.

In this book you'll find everything you need to know about cultivating the right lawn for your situation. Gain inspiration from the variety of lawns shown in the first chapter. Learn how to choose from among the many types of grass currently available. Finally, find out how efficient planting, watering, and maintenance practices can result in a healthy, verdant lawn that's a pleasure to behold.

For his invaluable and expert help with the manuscript and photographs, we wish to thank Dr. Ali Harivandi, Turfgrass Specialist, Cooperative Extension of Alameda County, University of California, Berkeley.

For their help with the text, we also thank Dr. M.C. Engelke, College of Agriculture, Texas A&M University, Dallas; Dr. Victor A. Gibeault, Extension Environmental Horticulturist, Department of Botany and Plant Sciences, University of California, Riverside; Dr. Anthony J. Koski, Assistant Professor of Turfgrass, Department of Horticulture, Colorado State University, Fort Collins; and Dr. William A. Meyer, Turf Seed, Inc., Hubbard, Oregon.

Special thanks also to Jim Borneman and Bob Pearson of Automatic Rain Company; Gus Selke of Cole & Weber; Russ Hayworth of Foster Turf; Bill Polk of Irrometer Company, Inc.; Jim Traub of Kensco Supply; John Holmquist and Dave Witzke of KKW, Inc.; Lou Sapudar and Mathew Narog of Lawn Clinic, Inc.; Madrone Landscape Group.

Also Orchard Supply Hardware; Ken Lyons, Cathy Morrow, and Kitty Tebrugge of Pursley Turf Farms; Dea L. Morrison of Rain Bird; Bill Trask of Sleepy Hollow Nursery; John McShane of Stover Seed Company; Rob Edelstein of Systematic Irrigation Controls, Inc.; Dennis Nord and Jack Prust of Toro; and Bill Stepka of Traditional Landscape Art.

Finally, we extend our thanks to Marianne Lipanovich for scouting and assistance with photography and to Scott Atkinson and Rod Smith for preliminary editorial research.

Book Editor
Fran Feldman

Research & Text
Michael Bowker

Contributing Editors
Gloria Mellinger
Lance Walheim
Susan Warton

Coordinating Editors
Deborah Thomas Kramer
Gregory J. Kaufman

Design
Joe di Chiarro

Illustrations
Jane McCreery

Photographers: Automatic Rain Company: 57 center left; Glenn Christiansen: 36; Roger DeWeese: 12 top; Derek Fell: 5, 6, 15 top; Horticultural Photography: 14 bottom; Michael Landis: 7 bottom, 8 top, 9 top left and bottom, 13, 27, 31, 60, 63, 65; Renee Lynn: 41 top left, bottom left, top right, bottom right, 67; Michael McKinley: 7 top, 10 bottom, 15 bottom; Norman A. Plate: 9 top right, 11; David Stubbs: 16; Michael S. Thompson: 1, 24; Darrow M. Watt: 10 top; Russ Widstrand: 28, 34, 42, 43, 46; Tom Wyatt: 8 bottom, 12 bottom, 14 top, 19, 20, 22, 23, 25, 26, 41 middle right, 49, 50, 51, 52, 53, 54, 55, 57 top, center right, and bottom, 58, 59.

Cover: Climbing roses, lavender blue clematis 'Ramona', and Dalmatian bellflower frame entryway leading to expansive lawn beyond. Cover design by Susan Bryant. Photography by Saxon Holt.

Editor, Sunset Books: Elizabeth L. Hogan

Second printing March 1994

Contents

Special Features

Lawns

Whether grown from seed
or sod, used for croquet or display, cultivated in a small plot
or a vast, rolling green, your lawn plays a prominent role in
your landscape. More than any other kind of greenery, lawns
are a basic fixture in residential gardens across a diverse
climatic range.

Although not hard to achieve, a healthy, lustrous carpet of
grass requires the right grass choices and a regular program
of watering and lawn care to sustain its green glory. A lawn's
appearance usually reflects the quality of its maintenance.
Basic feeding, watering, and mowing don't demand extensive
effort, but each task helps to create and preserve a beautiful,
flourishing lawn.

***Welcoming guests** into the garden, a carpet of
bluegrass displays the look of unabashed luxury
for which lawns are famous.*

Lawns
in the Landscape

Verdant Vistas

For garden-party glamor or a magnificent view, nothing can match the sweeping expanse of a picture-perfect, emerald green lawn.

***Stately home** requires a broad lawn to balance its imposing size. This one rolls richly over terraced slopes, contrasting with wide steps and walls of stone. Landscape architect: Thomas Church.*

***Keep off the grass?** That isn't always easy to enforce. Concrete squares provide an attractive alternative that protects St. Augustine blades as it directs foot traffic.*

***Swirling gracefully** between house, steps, and border plantings, this lush lawn is planted with perennial ryegrass cultivar Pennfine.*

Lawns in Miniature

Small-scale lawns create pockets of lush, cool green that require less upkeep and water. And they fit well on many urban and suburban lots.

Circle of tall fescue demands less water than a larger lawn would, yet still splashes vibrant color in an entry garden. *Landscape designer: Charlene Yockum.*

*A **swatch of green tall fescue*** *sets off paving, flowers, and foliage in a luxuriant patchwork landscape. Its velvety influence seems to soften adjacent driveway and garden path. Landscape designer: Richard Plaxco of Geared for Growing.*

Swath of bluegrass *sets off house and its landscaping from encircling border of trees, shrubs, ground covers, and blooms.*

A backyard oasis, *this curve of vivid fescue brightens a water-thrifty desert garden. Landscape designer: Ric Wogisch.*

Stepping-stones skip *across a 10-foot-wide lawn of bluegrass cultivar A-34, edged by brickwork and combined with drought-tolerant plantings. Design: Konrad Gauder of Landsculpture.*

Situational Problem Solvers

Lawns flow smoothly through complex landscapes, contributing design continuity and soft, rich texture as they also solve practical problems.

Cushioning turf under structure softens impact of falls. Rugged mix of Kentucky bluegrass and ryegrass handles foot traffic. Landscape design: Barbara Vendt, Con Mara Gardens. Play structure: Columbia Cascade.

Spreading trees shade carpet of lawn, an inviting place to linger on warm summer afternoons. Grass frames circular flower beds at bases of tree trunks. Landscape architect: Thomas Church.

Retaining walls cascade down a hillside garden to overlap this inviting lawn, used as a family play space. Landscape architect: John Herbst, Jr.

...Situational Problem Solvers

Flowing bluegrass visually calms and unites this complex garden, while accentuating its man-made dry creek bed and individual trees and shrubs. Landscape architect: DeWeese Burton Associates.

Serpentine curves and graceful slopes add interest to this spacious lawn; border plantings and path repeat undulating theme. Landscape architect: Peter Wright Shaw Associates, Inc.

Turf Innovations

More than just a smooth stretch of mowed grass, a lawn shows off its versatility when planted by an innovative gardener in surprising locations.

Hardscape meets softscape *in this unique garden walk that alternates bands of bluegrass with brickwork.*

Checkerboard hybrid *of lawn and patio results from planting tufts of grass inside open-ended concrete blocks. Grass grown here is a varietal called Warren turf A-34.*

Landscape Drama

With ribbons, circles, and other accents of green, decorative lawns show off nearby landscape elements to their brightest advantage.

__Island of green__ at center of a driveway, this plot of Kentucky bluegrass mixed with Bermuda grass dresses up surrounding pavement and provides a soft pad under swing. Landscape architect: James Chadwick.

__An emerald border__ outlining a stone-and-gravel path, this graceful lawn accents diverse foliage and flowers displayed along its edges.

Promenade of lawn, *a blend of bluegrass and ryegrass, draws stroller toward pergola. Vivid perennials border grassy path, heightening garden's drama.*

Rich greenery *enhances vibrant blooms of azaleas. Lawns often play role of a catalyst, making nearby flowers appear to explode with reds, yellows, or whites.*

Presenting the Grasses

Of the many hundreds of grasses that grow in the Northern Hemisphere, only about 40 types are usually cultivated as lawns. Many of those have numerous varieties developed to give you a multitude of choices.

Grasses vary greatly in their performance, appearance, watering needs, and maintenance requirements. Moreover, each grass has its own climate considerations. This chapter presents 18 of the most common grass types, each with a photo and description to help you make the right choice for your lawn.

Understanding Grasses

Grasses have these anatomical points in common: leaves grow alternately in two rows up the sides of jointed stems. The space between the joints may be hollow or pithy. A sheath surrounds the stem above each joint. Follow the sheath up and you come to a collarlike growth, the auricle, that clasps the stem at the top of the sheath. The blade grows outward, and usually upward, from this collar.

The particular arrangement of sheath, auricle, and blade helps botanists identify lawn grasses in the absence of flowers or a seed spike. Other aids to identification include the shape of the leaves, thickness of the stem, color, and means of spreading—stolons, or runners, above ground or rhizomes below ground.

Grass blades elongate from the lower end—when you mow off the tips, the leaves renew their length from the root end or new blades sprout from the base. This is why grasses perform so well as closely cropped ground covers.

Climate Considerations

The two basic kinds of grasses are cool season and warm season. Cool-season grasses withstand cold winters, but most types languish in hot summers. They're used mainly in northern latitudes.

Warm-season grasses grow vigorously during hot weather and go dormant in temperatures below freezing. If you find their winter brownness offensive, you can overseed (see page 18) with certain cool-season grasses. But grasses in the same group can perform differently in various climates. To choose the grass best adapted to your region, turn to the climate zone map on page 21. If you're unsure of the grass type you want or the best one for your area, consult a reputable nursery or your County Cooperative Extension office.

Cultivars, Blends & Mixtures

Lawns can be composed of a single grass type, called a cultivar, a blend, or a mixture. When a single *cultivar,* a grass that's named and grown on a regular basis for sale, is used, the lawn is the most uniform in appearance, giving you the maximum expression of whatever characteristic you select.

The main disadvantage of using a single type of grass is that it can be wiped out if it's susceptible to a pest or disease in the area.

Hardy Kentucky bluegrass *offers rich, deep color and high tolerance to cold.*

Using a *blend,* several cultivars of one species, or a *mixture,* composed of two or more different species, is safer. Seed companies prepare blends and mixtures for specific situations—one grass's strengths compensate for another's weaknesses in areas such as resistance to disease, drought tolerance, and wearability. Thus, a lawn can look good even when one grass type is suffering.

Overseeding

The major drawback of warm-season grasses is their unattractive dormancy during cool weather—they turn brown in winter. In many cases, cool-season grasses are seeded over warm-season grasses approaching dormancy. This maintains a green lawn all year but increases water use and maintenance.

Choosing a Grass

The following section presents the most common cool- and warm-season grasses. Dichondra is also included, although it isn't technically a grass. Native grasses, gaining in popularity because of their drought tolerance and low maintenance, are discussed on page 27.

With each grass description is a sampling of available cultivars. Not all the listed cultivars are available everywhere, and you may find additional ones in your area. Moreover, new named varieties appear on the market frequently; keep in mind that they may exhibit characteristics different from older cultivars.

A grass's root depth may be an important factor in your choice of grass type: shallow-rooted grasses need to be watered more often for shorter periods of time than deep-rooted grasses, which require deep watering less often.

In the grass descriptions that follow, "shallow" refers to roots up to 8 inches deep, "intermediate" to roots from 8 to 36 inches deep, and "deep" to roots deeper than 36 inches. These ranges refer to grass roots growing under ideal conditions and may vary a great deal depending on your maintenance practices.

Grasses at a Glance

For playing, running, or simply formal display, there's nothing comparable to a lush and healthy lawn. Cultivating such a lawn requires choosing the right grass type for your climate and your particular situation.

The chart below shows you at a glance each grass type's tolerance to certain conditions. For example, if you want a lawn that doesn't require massive amounts of water and chemicals, look for grasses with high tolerance to drought, pests, and disease. For a detailed description of each grass, refer to the individual listings that follow. To learn which grasses are best adapted to your climate, see the climate map on page 21.

	Tolerance to						
	Cold	Heat	Drought	Shade	Disease	Pests	Wear
Cool-season Grasses							
Colonial bent grass							
Creeping bent grass							
Kentucky bluegrass							
Rough-stalk bluegrass							
Chewings fescue							
Creeping red fescue							
Hard fescue							
Tall fescue							
Annual ryegrass							
Perennial ryegrass							
Warm-season Grasses							
Bahia grass							
Common Bermuda grass							
Hybrid Bermuda grass							
Centipede grass							
Dichondra							
Seashore paspalum							
St. Augustine grass							
Zoysia grass							

High   Moderate   Low

Bahia Grass

Paspalum notatum
Warm season

Introduced to the United States from Brazil in 1913, Bahia grass is a low-growing turf that spreads by runners. Its extensive, deep root system can help control erosion.

■ *Pluses:* Good in sandy or infertile soils. Tends to stay green longer in winter than other warm-season grasses. Some drought tolerance.

■ *Minuses:* Coarse and moderately aggressive; considered a weed in fine lawns. May turn yellow from chlorosis; dollar spot and mole crickets may also be problems. Frequent mowing required to remove seed heads.

■ *Regions:* Southeastern U.S. coastal areas, particularly Florida and the Gulf states.

■ *Sun/Shade:* Grows in sun or partial shade.

■ *Water:* Tolerates some drought but grows best with abundant water.

■ *Wear:* Very good wearability.

■ *Planting Methods:* Seed, sod.

■ *Mowing:* Mow 2 to 3 inches high; fast-growing seed stalks require frequent mowing.

■ *Fertilizer:* Apply ½ pound actual nitrogen per 1,000 square feet each month during active growing period.

■ *Cultivars:* Argentine, Paraguay, Pensacola.

Colonial Bent Grass

Agrostis tenuis
Cool season

Colonial bent grass is a fine-textured turf grass that produces high-quality lawns, ideal for golf course fairways. Its roots extend to an intermediate depth.

■ *Pluses:* Tolerates acidic, infertile soils and doesn't require much fertilizer. Also fairly drought tolerant.

■ *Minuses:* Does not perform well in extreme summertime heat. Depending on cultivar, is somewhat susceptible to pests and fungal diseases. Heavy thatch producer.

■ *Regions:* Coastal areas of northeastern U.S., Canada, Pacific Northwest, and California.

■ *Sun/Shade:* Needs sun but will tolerate moderate shade.

■ *Water:* Light to moderate watering required.

■ *Wear:* Moderate wearability.

■ *Planting Method:* Seed.

■ *Mowing:* Mow ½ to 1 inch high.

■ *Fertilizer:* Apply ⅛ to ¼ pound actual nitrogen per 1,000 square feet each month during active growing period.

■ *Cultivars:* Astoria, Bardot, Exeter.

Creeping Bent Grass

Agrostis palustris
Cool season

A fine-textured grass, creeping bent produces a high-quality lawn that, with constant care, is ideal for putting greens and lawn bowling. Its roots grow to an intermediate depth.

■ *Pluses:* Wears well and tolerates some heat.

■ *Minuses:* Needs ample water and constant care. More susceptible to pests and fungal disease than colonial bent.

■ *Regions:* Northeastern U.S. and Canada; coastal areas of Pacific Northwest and western Canada.

■ *Sun/Shade:* Likes full sun but will tolerate some shade.

■ *Water:* Frequent watering required.

■ *Wear:* Moderate wearability.

■ *Planting Method:* Seed.

■ *Mowing:* Mow ¼ to ½ inch high. Use a reel mower that's designed for close cutting.

■ *Fertilizer:* Apply ¼ to ½ pound actual nitrogen per 1,000 square feet each month during active growing period.

■ *Cultivars:* Emerald, Penncross, Penneagle, Pennlinks, Providence, Seaside.

Common Bermuda Grass

Cynodon dactylon
Warm season

Common Bermuda grass produces a medium- to fine-textured turf that spreads rapidly by surface and underground runners. This deep-rooted grass survives low maintenance, but extra care makes a more attractive lawn.

■ *Pluses:* Drought and heat tolerant; disease resistant. Outstanding wearability.

■ *Minuses:* Turns brown in winter but when well fertilized, some strains may remain green longer. Root system invasive if not confined; difficult to eradicate. Won't tolerate shade.

■ *Regions:* Southern U.S., Gulf Coast, and mild-weather western coastal areas.

■ *Sun/Shade:* Requires full sun. Poor shade tolerance.

■ *Water:* Needs less water than most grass types; tolerates drought well.

■ *Wear:* Excellent wearability.

■ *Planting Method:* Seed.

■ *Mowing:* Mow ¾ to 1 inch high, cutting ½ inch or less each time.

■ *Fertilizer:* Apply ½ to 1 pound actual nitrogen per 1,000 square feet each month during active growing period.

Hybrid Bermuda Grass

Cynodon
Warm season

Tough and heat loving, hybrid Bermuda grass makes a lawn that's finer textured and greener than common Bermuda grass. Tifway is a good cultivar for home lawns; Tifdwarf is best for golf greens. All are deep-rooted grasses.

■ *Pluses:* Drought tolerant. Very resistant to diseases and pests.

■ *Minuses:* Turns brown in winter. May tend to build up heavy thatch. Root system can be invasive. Won't tolerate shade.

■ *Regions:* Southern U.S., Gulf and East coasts, and mild-weather western coastal areas.

■ *Sun/Shade:* Requires full sun.

■ *Water:* Drought tolerant but needs regular watering to look good.

■ *Wear:* Excellent wearability.

■ *Planting Methods:* Sod, sprigs, plugs.

■ *Mowing:* Mow ½ to 1 inch high, cutting ½ inch or less each time. Use a reel mower. If allowed to grow longer, lawn tends to yellow.

■ *Fertilizer:* Apply ½ to 1 pound actual nitrogen per 1,000 square feet each month during active growing period. May require more for good appearance or recovery from wear.

■ *Cultivars:* Midiron, Midway, Ormond, Santa Ana, Sunturf, Tifdwarf, Tifgreen, Tiflawn, Tifway.

Kentucky Bluegrass

Poa pratensis
Cool season

A moderate- to fine-textured, hardy grass, Kentucky bluegrass is the most widely planted cool-season grass. Blue green in color, its blades have characteristic boat-shaped tips. Rhizomes of this shallow-rooted grass knit into firm turf.

■ *Pluses:* High cold tolerance. Many cultivars resistant to leaf spot, smut, and rust.

■ *Minuses:* Needs ample amounts of water. Some cultivars don't tolerate intense heat or shade.

■ *Regions:* Northern U.S. and Canada, and mountain and cool-weather areas of South and Southwest.

■ *Sun/Shade:* Likes full sun. Some cultivars tolerate a fair amount of shade.

■ *Water:* Requires frequent watering. Some cultivars won't tolerate drought conditions.

■ *Wear:* Moderate wearability.

■ *Planting Methods:* Seed, sod.

■ *Mowing:* Mow 1½ to 2 inches high.

■ *Fertilizer:* Apply ½ to 1 pound actual nitrogen per 1,000 square feet during active growing period. Some improved, established varieties do well with less.

■ *Cultivars:* Adelphi, America, A-34, Bristol, Challenger, Cheri, Columbia, Eclipse, Glade, Kenblue, Majestic, Midnight, Newport, Nugget, Parade, Plush, Rugby, Sydsport, Touchdown, Vantage, Windsor.

Climate Map for Grasses

The map below is divided into seven climate zones, each of which is characterized by particular climate conditions. Grasses that grow well in each zone are listed.

Keep in mind that the map is only a guide. Specific areas within a zone may vary in rainfall, temperature, altitude, terrain, and soil. Areas bordering the dividing lines are transitional: the grasses that flourish in those areas may be different from those that do well throughout the rest of the region. For help, consult your local nursery or County Co-operative Extension office.

■ *ZONE 1: West and Pacific Northwest.* Climate is cool and humid. Rain is plentiful, except during summer in West. Lawns seeded from cool-season grasses—bent grasses, fine and tall fescues, Kentucky bluegrass, and perennial ryegrass—do well in this area.

■ *ZONE 2: Southwest.* Temperatures arc high. Rainfall is scarce and soils are dry. Lawns here need additional irrigation. Bermuda grass is used primarily, with some zoysia and St. Augustine. With adequate irrigation, tall fescue can provide year-round turf where temperatures are not too severe. Dichondra is used in Southern California. Perennial ryegrass is excellent for winter overseeding of dormant warm-season grasses.

■ *ZONE 3: Mountains, Great Plains, and Central Plains of Canada.* Climate is dry and semiarid, with wide temperature fluctuations. Drought-tolerant native grasses (buffalo grass, crested wheatgrass, and blue grama) do well. With irrigation, fine fescues and Kentucky and rough-stalk bluegrasses succeed in northern areas, and tall fescue (and occasionally Bermuda and zoysia) in southern areas. Dichondra does well in mild-winter western areas.

■ *ZONE 4: Northeastern U. S. and Eastern Canada.* Summers are hot and humid, winters cold and snowy. Rainfall is abundant and soils are often acidic. Colonial and creeping bent grasses, Kentucky and rough-stalk bluegrasses, and perennial and annual ryegrasses are common; fine fescues are used in northern areas.

■ *ZONE 5: North and South.* Summers are warm and humid, with abundant rainfall. Winters are generally mild but can be severe. Bermuda grass, tall fescue, and zoysia grass perform well. Kentucky and rough-stalk bluegrasses and perennial and annual ryegrasses also are used.

■ *ZONE 6: Central South.* Climate is warm and humid with abundant rainfall; winters are mild. Bermuda grass, centipede grass, tall fescue, and zoysia do well. Kentucky bluegrass is used in cooler areas, St. Augustine in southern areas.

■ *ZONE 7: Florida, Gulf Coast, and Hawaii.* Climate is semitropical to tropical with a year-round growing season. Rainfall is generally very high. Bahia, Bermuda, centipede, St. Augustine, and zoysia grasses grow well throughout most of the region. Bent grasses, fine fescues, and ryegrasses are useful for winter overseeding of dormant warm-season turfs.

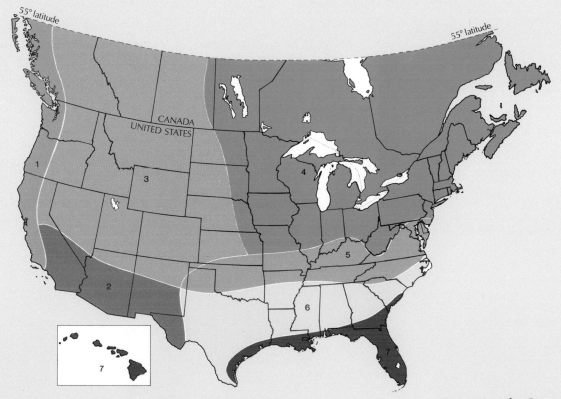

Rough-stalk Bluegrass

Poa trivialis
Cool season

Rough-stalk bluegrass is a bright green, fine-textured turf. Like Kentucky bluegrass, its blades have boat-shaped tips. A shallow-rooted grass, it does well in wet, shady areas. Some recommend its use in mixtures, but it may become weedy.

■ *Pluses:* Outstanding shade tolerance. Minimal fertilizer requirements.

■ *Minuses:* Needs ample amounts of water. Poor wearability. Can turn yellow during cool periods and develop brown spots in summer. Susceptible to fungal diseases. Can become a weed in wet soil.

■ *Regions:* Northern U.S. and Canada, and mountain and cool-weather areas of South and Southwest.

■ *Sun/Shade:* Outstanding shade tolerance.

■ *Water:* Requires frequent watering. Doesn't tolerate drought conditions.

■ *Wear:* Poor wearability.

■ *Planting Method:* Seed.

■ *Mowing:* Mow 1½ to 2 inches high.

■ *Fertilizer:* Apply ¼ to ½ pound actual nitrogen per 1,000 square feet each month during active growing period.

■ *Cultivars:* Colt, Laser, Sabre.

Centipede Grass

Eremochloa ophiuroides
Warm season

This light green, medium- to fine-textured grass spreads by stolons, crowding out weeds. Its root depth varies from shallow to deep.

■ *Pluses:* Does well in infertile or acidic soils. Requires little maintenance. Resistant to chinch bugs and rhizoctonia.

■ *Minuses:* Vulnerable to chlorosis. Poor wear and cold-weather tolerance; cold causes browning.

■ *Regions:* Southeastern U.S., Gulf Coast, and Hawaii.

■ *Sun/Shade:* Likes full sun but tolerates some shade.

■ *Water:* Requires frequent watering. Shallow-rooted varieties not drought tolerant.

■ *Wear:* Takes only light wear; shallow-rooted types damage easily.

■ *Planting Methods:* Seed, sod, sprigs, plugs.

■ *Mowing:* Mow 1 to 2 inches high.

■ *Fertilizer:* Apply less than ¼ pound actual nitrogen per 1,000 square feet during active growing period. Don't overfertilize.

■ *Cultivars:* Centennial, Centiseed, Oklawn.

Dichondra

Dichondra micrantha
Warm season

A perennial lawn plant or ground cover, dichondra is a soft, bright green, ground-hugging plant that behaves like a grass. It produces a lush mat of small, broad leaves that resemble miniature lily pads. Shallow rooted, it spreads by rooting surface runners.

■ *Pluses:* Looks thick and luxurious. Depending on desired appearance, can be mowed infrequently. Will tolerate heat and some shade.

■ *Minuses:* Needs ample amounts of water and constant vigilance against such pests as cutworms, flea beetles, snails, and slugs. Weeds are difficult to eradicate and can be invasive.

■ *Regions:* Mild-winter areas of western and southwestern U.S.

■ *Sun/Shade:* Likes full sun but tolerates some shade.

■ *Water:* Requires frequent, thorough watering, which encourages deep root growth and increases drought tolerance.

■ *Wear:* Tolerates ordinary lawn traffic, not heavy play.

■ *Planting Methods:* Seed, sod, plugs.

■ *Mowing:* Mow ¾ to 2 inches high.

■ *Fertilizer:* Apply ½ to 1 pound actual nitrogen per 1,000 square feet each month during active growing period.

Chewings Fescue

Festuca rubra commutata
Cool season

Chewings fescue is an aggressive, bunch-type fine fescue that can overtake other grasses. It's very tolerant of shade and mixes well with Kentucky bluegrass. Its roots grow to an intermediate depth.

■ *Pluses:* Good for overseeding shady areas of dormant Bermuda grass when mixed with perennial ryegrass. Excellent shade tolerance. Good drought tolerance.

■ *Minuses:* Vulnerable to fungal diseases during spells of hot, wet weather. Poor wearability; slow to reestablish after root damage.

■ *Regions:* Northern U.S. and Canada, and cooler elevations elsewhere. Particularly adapted to cool coastal areas of Northeast and Pacific Northwest.

■ *Sun/Shade:* Excellent shade tolerance.

■ *Water:* Not especially thirsty. Drought tolerant.

■ *Wear:* Takes only very light traffic.

■ *Planting Method:* Seed.

■ *Mowing:* Mow 1 to 2½ inches high.

■ *Fertilizer:* Apply ¼ to ½ pound actual nitrogen per 1,000 square feet each month during active growing period. Don't overfertilize.

■ *Cultivars:* Banner, Enjoy, Highlight, Jamestown, Longfellow, Mary, Shadow, Tamara, Victory.

Creeping Red Fescue

Festuca rubra rubra
Cool season

A fine-textured fescue, creeping red has narrow, dark green blades. It grows well on slopes and banks, creating a lush effect when not mowed. Planted alone, it grows in clumps; in mixtures, it compensates for weaknesses in other grasses. Roots grow to intermediate depth.

■ *Pluses:* Most shade tolerant of good lawn grasses. Where winter wear is limited, good for overseeding dormant warm-season grasses. Drought tolerant.

■ *Minuses:* Poor wearability; slow to recover when damaged. Vulnerable to fungal diseases during hot, wet weather. Spreads slowly.

■ *Regions:* Northern U.S. and Canada, and high elevations elsewhere. Good in cool coastal areas of Northeast and Pacific Northwest.

■ *Sun/Shade:* Excellent shade tolerance.

■ *Water:* Low to moderate watering needs; overwatering encourages disease. Drought tolerant.

■ *Wear:* Poor wearability.

■ *Planting Method:* Seed.

■ *Mowing:* Mow 1½ to 2½ inches high.

■ *Fertilizer:* Apply ¼ to ½ pound actual nitrogen per 1,000 square feet each month during active growing period. Don't overfertilize.

■ *Cultivars:* Boreal, Dawson, Ensylva, Flyer, Fortress, Illahee, Pennlawn, Pernille, Ruby, Shademaster.

Hard Fescue

Festuca longifolia
Cool season

A clumping, fine-textured grass, hard fescue grows more slowly than other fescues, requires little maintenance, and mixes well with other grasses. Its roots reach an intermediate depth.

■ *Pluses:* Excellent shade and drought tolerance; does well even in poor soil. Good disease resistance. Newer cultivars mow well; can also be left unmowed as a ground cover.

■ *Minuses:* Some cultivars are difficult to mow evenly; shredded tips can discolor.

■ *Regions:* Northern U.S. and Canada, and high elevations elsewhere. Particularly adapted to cool coastal areas of Northeast and Pacific Northwest.

■ *Sun/Shade:* Excellent shade tolerance.

■ *Water:* Very drought tolerant. Don't overwater.

■ *Wear:* Moderate wearability. Clumps recover slowly from damage.

■ *Planting Method:* Seed.

■ *Mowing:* Mow 1½ to 2½ inches high; or leave unmowed.

■ *Fertilizer:* Apply ¼ to ½ pound actual nitrogen per 1,000 square feet during active growing period. Don't overfertilize.

■ *Cultivars:* Aurora, Reliant, Scaldis, Spartan, Tournament, Waldina.

Tough Turf for Play Surfaces

For most people, the scent of bruised grass brings on a flood of memories—twilight games of hide-and-seek, the absorbing joy of a close volleyball game, the crack of a bat followed by the lazy hiss of a grounder.

Turf is everyone's favorite activity surface. It's springy, resilient, and renewable, and it even smells good. Yet many lawns are underutilized because their owners think only about appearance, forgetting that grass can be hard-working and still look great.

Planning a play area. As you design your landscape, consider how best to use the different areas around your home. You may want to keep the portion visible to the outside world ornamental and use back or side sections for sport. Be sure to keep in mind the proximity of trees and shrubs to activity areas—shade will affect the grass choice, and overhanging branches can snare balls and birdies.

Durable and attractive, *perennial ryegrass stands up to wear, performs well on play surfaces.*

The choice of a grass variety or blend will depend on climate, sun-shade ratio, and, of course, the sport at hand. In general, any wear-resistant grass can do recreational duty, although some grasses are better for specific applications than others. For example, the fine texture of colonial bent grass makes it an excellent choice for a putting green, but any harder use would destroy it.

The most desirable quality in a sporting turf is the ability to rebound quickly from damage. Drought resistance, moderate thatch (for resilience), deep roots, and density are other desirable characteristics.

Best bets. Among the favorite turf grasses for athletic surfaces are warm-season Bermuda and zoysia grasses and cool-season perennial ryegrass and tall fescue.

■ *Bermuda grass* is perhaps the most widely adaptable athletic turf grass; it's used on baseball fields, golf course fairways, and football fields. Resistant to drought, pests, and disease, Bermuda grass is tough and deep rooted. Its major drawback is low shade tolerance.

■ *Zoysia grass* may be a better choice than Bermuda for shady yards. A heat-loving turf grass, zoysia is dense, fine textured, and drought tolerant. It wears almost as well as Bermuda grass but turns brown sooner in areas with cool fall weather.

■ *Perennial ryegrass,* a cool-season grass, is also a good choice for recreational use. It offers excellent wearability and moderate shade tolerance.

■ *Tall fescue* is a cool-season grass that stays green the year around, is a fairly tough surface, and tolerates a moderate amount of shade. The recent development of newer, nonclumping cultivars with greater drought tolerance than older ones has made tall fescue a very popular surface for play areas.

Other hard-working turf grasses. Other grasses work well in certain situations, although they may not be the most desirable types for athletic surfaces.

One of these is bahia grass, a warm-season grass that has an expansive, deep root system. Because of this, it's good for unstable slopes and loose soils in large play areas. It tolerates a fair amount of shade and stays green longer than other warm-season grasses. However, it doesn't form a very dense turf, and the tall seed stalks require frequent mowing.

Tall Fescue

Festuca arundinacea
Cool season

Tall fescue is a dense grass that stays green year-round. It's used for play areas and athletic surfaces. Newer cultivars tend to be less coarse and more attractive than older ones and are used for lawns.

■ *Pluses:* More heat tolerant than other cool-season grasses. Will survive drought conditions longer and better than bluegrass or perennial ryegrass. Some resistance to disease and pests.

■ *Minuses:* Some cultivars considered a fast-growing weed in mixtures. May go dormant in cold winters.

■ *Regions:* Transitional zones with mild winters and warm summers; in mild-temperature regions of Southwest.

■ *Sun/Shade:* Moderate shade tolerance.

■ *Water:* Needs infrequent, deep watering but does well under drought conditions.

■ *Wear:* High wearability.

■ *Planting Methods:* Seed, sod.

■ *Mowing:* Mow 1½ to 2 inches high for athletic use; otherwise, mow 2 to 3 inches high.

■ *Fertilizer:* Apply ¼ to ½ pound actual nitrogen per 1,000 square feet during active growing period.

■ *Cultivars:* Adventure, Apache, Arid, Bonanza, Bonsai, Falcon, Jaguar, Marathon, Olympic, Pacer, Rebel, Tempo, Trailblazer, Trident.

Seashore Paspalum

Paspalum vaginatum
Warm season

This glossy, deep green, medium-textured grass is native to Australia. It was introduced to the United States as an alternative to Bermuda grass in dry coastal areas.

■ *Pluses:* Spreads quickly but is easy to contain. Requires little maintenance. Tolerant of heat, drought, and salty soils. Resistant to pests.

■ *Minuses:* Browns during cold weather. Produces tough stems in late summer that turn brown after scalping.

■ *Regions:* Cool coastal areas of Southern California.

■ *Sun/Shade:* Likes full sun but tolerates some shade.

■ *Water:* Requires a moderate amount of water (more than Bermuda grass).

■ *Wear:* Good wearability.

■ *Planting Method:* Sod.

■ *Mowing:* Mow ¾ to 1 inch high.

■ *Fertilizer:* Apply ½ to ¾ pound actual nitrogen per 1,000 square feet each month during active growing period.

■ *Cultivars:* Adalayd (Excalibre), Futurf.

Annual Ryegrass

Lolium multiflorum
Cool season

Annual ryegrass, though coarse in texture, is used for overseeding dormant warm-season grasses, providing an attractive alternative to brown lawns from fall to late spring; most die out with heat. Roots are shallow.

■ *Pluses:* Germinates and establishes quickly. When mixed with slower germinating varieties, it offers protection from wind and foot traffic while other varieties are becoming established.

■ *Minuses:* Clumping makes an uneven surface; rapid growth rate requires frequent mowing. Can become weedy. Intolerant of extremes in temperature. Requires frequent watering.

■ *Regions:* Good in transitional climate zones with mild winters and warm summers, and in South, Northeast, and Pacific Northwest.

■ *Sun/Shade:* Likes full sun. Poor shade tolerance.

■ *Water:* Moderate to high water requirement. Not drought tolerant.

■ *Wear:* Moderate wearability.

■ *Planting Method:* Seed.

■ *Mowing:* Mow 1½ to 2 inches high.

■ *Fertilizer:* Apply ¼ to ½ pound actual nitrogen per 1,000 square feet each month during active growing period.

■ *Cultivars:* Agree and Oregreen (hybrids of annual and perennial ryegrasses).

Perennial Ryegrass

Lolium perenne
Cool season

Shallow rooted with deep green, glossy blades, perennial ryegrass has a finer texture than annual ryegrass. Because it establishes itself quickly, it, too, is used to overseed warm-season lawns.

■ *Pluses:* Outstanding wearability. Fast germination and quick growth.

■ *Minuses:* Fibrous leaves on some cultivars tear when mowed, but improved cultivars mow cleanly. Can delay germination of other grasses. Sensitive to extreme cold and heat.

■ *Regions:* Cool-climate areas of Midwest and West, and coastal areas of Northeast.

■ *Sun/Shade:* Likes full sun but tolerates some shade.

■ *Water:* Requires frequent watering.

■ *Wear:* Excellent wearability.

■ *Planting Methods:* Seed, sod.

■ *Mowing:* Mow 1½ to 2 inches high.

■ *Fertilizer:* Apply ¼ to ½ pound actual nitrogen per 1,000 square feet each month during active growing period.

■ *Cultivars:* All Star, Birdie II, Blazer II, Dasher II, Derby, Diplomat, Fiesta, Gator, Loretta, Manhattan II, Omega II, Palmer, Pennant, Pennfine, Prelude, Regal, Tara, Yorktown II.

St. Augustine Grass

Stenotaphrum secundatum
Warm season

This deep-rooted, extremely coarse-textured grass with broad, dark green blades spreads rapidly by surface runners that root at the joints. New cultivars are finer textured.

■ *Pluses:* The most shade tolerant of all the warm-season grasses. Aggressive, crowds out most weeds. Tolerates steady traffic and salty conditions. Excellent heat resistance.

■ *Minuses:* Can produce heavy thatch. Some varieties susceptible to chinch bugs and St. Augustine grass decline (SAD) virus. Looks ragged in winter.

■ *Regions:* Coastal areas of Southeast, Gulf states, Florida, and Southern California.

■ *Sun/Shade:* Will grow in sun. Tolerates even dense shade well.

■ *Water:* Requires frequent watering.

■ *Wear:* Takes hard use.

■ *Planting Methods:* Sod, sprigs, plugs.

■ *Mowing:* Mow 1½ to 2 inches high; use a reel mower. If mowed too low, weeds can be a problem.

■ *Fertilizer:* Apply ½ to 1 pound actual nitrogen per 1,000 square feet each month during active growing period.

■ *Cultivars:* Bitter Blue, Floratine, Floratum, Seville, Sunclipse.

Zoysia Grass

Zoysia species
Warm season

Zoysia grass is fine textured with wiry blades. Deep rooted, it spreads slowly by creeping rhizomes and stolons to make a dense turf. Some cultivars make good play surfaces.

■ *Pluses:* Good resistance to most pests except billbugs; very good drought and heat tolerance. Very attractive when well tended.

■ *Minuses:* Slow to get established and propagate, although newer types spread faster. Goes dormant sooner than other warm-season grasses and may stay brown longer.

■ *Regions:* Southern U.S. coastal areas and Southern California.

■ *Sun/Shade:* Moderate shade tolerance.

■ *Water:* Low water requirement once established. Drought tolerant.

■ *Wear:* Good wearability.

■ *Planting Methods:* Sod, sprigs, plugs.

■ *Mowing:* Mow 1 to 2 inches high.

■ *Fertilizer:* Apply ¼ to ½ pound actual nitrogen per 1,000 square feet each month during active growing period.

■ *Cultivars:* Bel Air, El Toro, Emerald, Jade, Meyer, Midwest, Sunburst.

A Selection of Native Grasses

Native grasses, unlike the more commonly used turf grasses, are indigenous to North America. Because they haven't been bred for uniformity like the introduced species, they exhibit variations in height and color, and look more natural and informal in the landscape.

Although not used historically on lawns, native grasses are gaining in popularity because of their tolerance to drought and low maintenance requirements. They need to be watered from germination to establishment, but once established, require minimal watering, fertilizing, and mowing. They also help control wind and water erosion by stabilizing loose earth, so they're useful on hillsides and banks.

Native grasses are green only during their growing season, which can be rather short, and don't offer the high quality of the more traditional turf grasses.

Beach grass (*Ammophila breviligulata*) is an erect, hardy grass that grows well in coastal areas, on dunes and beaches, and in sandy, arid soils inland. It establishes deep roots and spreads widely by underground rhizomes. Its leaves are tough and coarse.

Blue grama (*Bouteloua gracilis*) is a hardy, pale green pasture grass with slightly fuzzy blades. It tolerates wide temperature fluctuations and thrives in the arid, windy areas of the Central Plains states. It's very drought tolerant and requires little maintenance.

Blue grama offers moderate wearability but recovers slowly from damage. It's slow to germinate and become established, and goes dormant in hot weather.

Buffalo grass (*Buchloe dactyloides*) has great potential as a lawn grass; current research in many areas of the country is yielding ever-improving cultivars that make buffalo grass competitive with many of the established turf grasses.

Buffalo grass is a pale, fine-textured prairie grass that germinates quickly and makes a dense sod. It survives intense heat but turns golden in winter. Other advantages that make buffalo grass a potential favorite include excellent drought tolerance, very good wearability, and low maintenance requirements. Because it only grows to 4 to 5 inches in height, it needs very little mowing.

Buffalo grass is indigenous to the prairie states and to Texas and Arizona, but it can be grown elsewhere. Because of its shallow roots, it does well where there are frequent, short afternoon rains. It grows well in alkaline soils but doesn't like sandy soils.

Crested wheatgrass (*Agropyron cristatum*), a light bluish green, medium-textured grass, grows well in mountainous areas and is used extensively for roadside erosion control in Colorado. It germinates fairly quickly and grows successfully in a wide range of climates, from extremely hot to below freezing. It prefers some moisture but will survive drought, and is adapted to alkaline soils.

Crested wheatgrass grows in thick clumps. It goes dormant and turns brown in hot weather.

Carpet of buffalo grass *survives on rainfall. A deep irrigation in spring greens it up; one in fall keeps it growing later in year.*

Planting a Lawn

Verdant, emerald green expanses of lawn are so commonplace in the landscape that it's hard not to take them for granted. In cities, they offer a restful contrast to the miles of paving that assault the eyes and bring special beauty to a hard-edged landscape. In small towns, they link structures one to another and contribute to a feeling of openness and warmth.

But it's important to remember that planting a lawn—whether you're starting from scratch or replacing an existing lawn—is a project that requires an investment of time and money, as well as a firm commitment to conscientious maintenance.

Is it worth it? You bet. Turf is beautiful, useful, and, if installed and maintained correctly, fully in keeping with the new spirit of water conservation. It will help to improve the quality of life for you and your family for many years to come.

In fact, preparing soil and planting grass is well within the ability of the average home owner who's willing to put some time and energy into the task. All of the steps, as outlined in this chapter, are straightforward and not difficult. As you read, remember that the two most important keys to success are good planning and attention to detail.

Getting Started

It's important to be realistic about the amount of time and money you're willing to spend on planting your lawn. Even if you decide to do most of the work yourself, you may want to call in a landscaping professional for advice on specific issues—for example, on the types of grasses that grow well in your local area. A professional can also advise you on how to deal with any grading or soil problems.

Working with Professionals

You can choose from a number of qualified lawn experts, including landscape architects, landscape designers, landscape contractors, nursery personnel, and professional gardeners. Most professionals can be hired on a limited or hourly basis.

Regardless of whom you approach, look for evidence that the person listens carefully to your ideas and problems and is responsive to them. It's always a good idea to ask for references and talk to former clients. Try to see some of the professional's work, if possible. It's also best to get more than one estimate if the cost will be significant.

If you hire someone to plant your lawn and do the necessary preparation work, you'll probably want to have a clear contract for specified services, including guarantees that your design will be followed and that work will be completed by a certain date. One way to ensure the promptness of the work is to include a per-day late penalty clause in the contract. Before the professional team begins work, check with your in-

(Continued on page 32)

***Pallets of freshly cut sod** await installation. With sod, you can transform bare earth into a lush green lawn in just a few hours.*

A Lawn Design Primer

Grass is one of the most common plants in the landscape. By itself, a single grass plant seems innocuous and, in fact, rather plain. But there is strength in numbers. Thousands of plants together form one of our oldest friends—the grass lawn.

A lawn does more than cover up dirt. A cool green expanse of grass, with its uniform texture and color, bestows a polished look on any patch of ground. It makes the structures around it look better, too. There's a certain formality to a lawn that's pleasing to the eye as well as the senses.

You'll seldom have an opportunity to be so creative, or to enjoy such practical, long-term benefits from your creativity, as when you plan and design a new lawn and landscape, or remodel an old one. A vital, functioning landscape transcends mere decoration to become a unique expression of your personality and life-style.

Careful planning at the design stage is the key to achieving the effect that will make a difference between a plain lawn and one that is graceful, fits into the surrounding landscape, and meets your family's needs. Creating a good design takes attention to some basic design principles and clear thinking about your needs.

Basic Landscaping Principles

A lawn doesn't have to be a simple square or rectangle, with four perfectly straight sides. As the photographs in "Lawns in the Landscape" on pages 7–15 demonstrate, lawns and plantings can take different shapes. For example, you may want to design a nearly circular lawn surrounded by plantings, such as the one shown on the facing page. Or you can curve a lawn to follow the lines of a freeform swimming pool. Let your imagination—and good design sense—experiment with different shapes and sizes.

Keep in mind that whether you're planning a large, formal landscape or something much more modest, observing the four basic landscaping principles will ensure that your entire garden design is visually pleasing.

Unity. A unified landscape is all of one piece, rather than disjointed groupings and scatterings of features. No one element stands out; instead, all the parts work together.

Strong, observable lines and the repetition of geometric shapes contribute significantly to the unity of your landscape, as does simplicity—for example, using just a few harmonious colors and a limited number of plant varieties. Be prepared to give up the idea of having every one of your favorite plants around you and avoid designing too many distinct units that will have to be tied together.

Start with your lawn; think of it as a neutral element, a blank canvas on which you'll assemble your landscaping units to provide balance, proportion, and variety.

Balance. To balance a landscape is to use mass, color, or form to create equal visual weight on either side of a center of interest. In a formal landscape, balance may mean simply creating one side as a mirror image of the other.

In informal styles, balance is just as important, but more subtle: a large tree to the left of an entryway can be balanced by a grouping of smaller trees on the right. Likewise, you can balance a concentration of color in a small flower bed on one side of a lawn with a much larger and more diffuse mass of greenery on the other side.

Proportion. In a well-designed landscape, the various structural and plant elements are in scale with one another. Start with your house; it will largely determine proportion in your landscape. When choosing trees and shrubs, keep their ultimate sizes and shapes in mind.

Variety. Break up a monotonous landscape by selecting plants in a variety of shapes, shades, and textures; or add interest by juxtaposing different materials.

Designing for Practicality

As you think about the design of your lawn and plantings, try to be perfectly clear about what you want your landscape to give you, and what you're prepared to give it. Whatever you plant now will have to be maintained for many years to come. Don't make the mistake of sowing the seeds of a shade-intolerant grass in an area where the sun cannot easily penetrate. (For help in identifying the characteristics of various grasses, see the chapter beginning on page 17.)

Organizing space. Patterns of turf around your house can both accommodate and display other plants. Low and lush, grass is the perfect foil for flowering trees and shrubs, as well as for bright annuals or perennials. Grass also draws the eye around a landscape and is the perfect space organizer—you can shape it to help define an area or direct traffic around it.

Keep off the grass? If you have young children, don't think that you'll be able to keep them and the neighborhood kids off your lawn. Instead, choose a grass that will stand up to wear and recover quickly from injury or abuse. Likewise, if you expect to entertain frequently out-of-doors, make sure your grass can take the additional wear and tear.

Your natural environment. Don't try to fight your environment by choosing plantings that, although attractive, are unsuited to your microclimate.

Although soil can be amended and improved (as explained in this chapter) if it lacks certain nutrients or suffers from a bad grade or poor drainage, there's not much you can do if you live in an area where rainfall is scarce. With today's emphasis on water conservation, due in part to recurring drought conditions and in part to a simple shortage of water to serve increasing populations, choosing drought-tolerant grasses and plantings is essential. The availability of a myriad of grass cultivars means that you can plant a grass both you and your microclimate can live with.

Think also, while you're still in the planning stage, about your water delivery system (see pages 47–59). Now is the perfect time to put in an underground sprinkler system. Or are you satisfied to use a simple hose and hose-end sprinkler? If you're irrigating by hand, you may want to keep your lawn area small for ease of watering.

If towering trees dot your landscape, plant a grass type that's appropriate for the amount of shade they cast. Remember, too, that grass will compete with tree roots for available water and nutrients, so you may have to water more deeply and fertilize more often.

Thinking about lawn care. A lovely lawn need not make a slave of its owner. If you much prefer playing a set of tennis to mowing the front lawn, be selective about the type of grass you plant. Some require more frequent mowing than others.

The same is true of other gardening chores. Grasses that are disease and insect resistant will require less care than grasses that aren't. Fertilizer requirements vary, too.

Structural elements. Designing mowing strips and other edgings (see page 48) along the perimeter of your lawn will make lawn management easier. A mowing strip accommodates the wheels of your mower, enabling you to cut right to the edge of the grass and eliminating trimming chores.

Edgings neatly contain your lawn—and any plantings on the other side. If you plant a grass that grows by stolons, or runners, edgings will help keep growth within bounds.

Small circle of lawn ringed by trees and low-growing plants offers shade and color, as well as play space. Landscape designer: Alan Rollinger.

(Continued from page 29)

surance agent to find out who is liable in case of injury or property damage.

Most professional companies will require a deposit before they'll begin any work on your property, but before you make the final payment, be sure the job has been completed to your satisfaction.

The following professionals offer expertise in specialized areas.

Landscape architects hold one or more degrees in their field and are trained and often licensed to design both commercial and residential landscapes. Many are willing to offer you a simple consultation, either in their office or at your home, for a modest fee.

Landscape architects alone are licensed to prepare designs for a fee, which may be an hourly rate, a flat sum, or a percentage of construction costs.

Landscape designers usually limit themselves to residential landscape design. They're unlicensed and meet no specific educational requirements, although many are extremely skilled and experienced. In some states they're barred from certain kinds of structural designing.

Landscape contractors are trained, and in some states licensed, to install landscapes, including plantings, pavings, structures, and irrigation systems. Some also offer design services, which may be included in the total price of materials and installation. They can also interpret and implement the plans of a landscape architect.

Nursery personnel often provide design services, usually at no charge if you buy their plants. In addition, some nurseries have highly skilled personnel who are available for outside consultations or who are able to recommend good local professionals.

Professional gardeners may do everything from mowing and raking to planting and highly skilled maintenance; fees vary accordingly. There is no special training required for gardeners. In some states, gardeners are prohibited from installing landscapes unless their fees fall below a certain limit.

Legal Considerations

Your city or county building department personnel can help you determine which codes and ordinances will affect your landscaping plans, and what permits and inspections are required. If you're simply planting a lawn, you probably won't need a permit.

Laying a Solid Foundation

As in any building project, constructing a solid foundation—in this case, a seedbed—is essential to creating a long-lasting lawn.

If you're replacing an existing lawn, you'll first have to get rid of all of the old grass. The most efficient way to do this is to kill the existing turf and weeds with a broad spectrum herbicide, such as glyphosate. Once the lawn material is dead, you can work it into the soil with a power tiller.

If you're starting your lawn from scratch, however, the first step involves grading your soil—moving soil so it's at the proper height and slope to ensure adequate drainage for the lawn.

Improving drainage by working with the soil to channel and collect excess water away from the lawn is the next step—and one that's often overlooked by gardeners preparing their own lawn seedbeds.

Here's a closer look at those steps. Even if you don't do this work yourself, it's important to understand the process so you can make sure the company you hire is doing it right.

Grading

The work of grading progresses hand-in-hand with the other aspects of installing your landscape. Generally, you'll need to begin with rough grading, bringing the areas of your yard to the desired finished level. Then, after you've installed any underground watering system, you'll need to re-establish the rough grade. The final stage is the finish grading.

If the grading is simple and you have the time and inclination to do it, you can save money and have the satisfaction of having literally shaped the land you'll live with for years to come. But many special situations require that you obtain professional help or, at least, advice.

For example, if an area around existing trees is to be graded, call in a tree expert who understands how to grade without damaging the trees. If steep or unstable slopes are to be smoothed out, call in a landscape architect or civil engineer—someone who can foresee all the implications and who is familiar with legal requirements. In short, rely on the expertise of professionals for major grading of any unstable area.

If your landscape is nearly flat, be sure that it has adequate surface drainage: a minimum slope of nearly 3 inches per 10 feet of unpaved ground. A steeper gradient is better for slow-draining, heavy soils. Also be sure that runoff is directed away from adjacent property and toward a storm sewer or drainage ditch.

Before you start digging, check with your building department for any permits you may need. When you're digging, it's essential to know the location of any underground lines for gas, water, sewer, electricity, telephone, or other utilities. If your home isn't connected to a sewer, locate the septic tank and drainage field.

Rough Grading

The goal of rough grading is to remove or add enough soil in each area of your yard to bring the soil surface to the height and slope you want, thus ensuring proper water drainage.

Eliminating high spots. Excavate any high places in your yard so the level of the soil will be at the desired height and slope. When you dig, put the topsoil (usually the top 6 to 8 inches of soil) and subsoil in separate piles. You'll use them later for filling.

Filling low spots. Fill low spots in your yard by adding soil to bring the level up to the desired height and slope. Partially fill any deep holes with subsoil, leaving room for a final layer of topsoil so plants can grow. Use just topsoil to fill shallow areas.

Getting the Grade You Want

As you grade, you'll need a reliable method to ensure that you get the grade you want. During rough grading, you can simply estimate the grade visually; for greater accuracy, use a carpenter's level.

Visually estimating. Establishing the grade by "eye-balling" is often all that's required. Inspect the grade closely to be sure any slope goes in the proper direction—away from structures and toward areas where water can drain away without causing problems. Also look for high and low spots.

Estimating with a level. Using a level is more accurate than visually estimating. Set the level on an 8-foot-long 2 by 4 placed on the ground. With a tape measure, determine how far you have to raise one end of the board to center the bubble in the level. That way you can get a rough idea of how much the ground slopes.

Improving Drainage

Good drainage is vital for growing healthy lawns. Methods for solving drainage problems range from the relatively easy one of improving the composition of the soil to more complex solutions that include digging trenches or installing a drainage chimney, dry well, or catch basin.

Unless your lawn has obvious topographical problems, consider the simple solutions first.

Working with the Soil

Grading the soil for the proper slope, as explained at left, is a basic way to improve drainage. Sometimes, this will eliminate all drainage problems. But if you have a layer of hardpan, or tight, compacted soil, in your yard, you'll need to take more drastic action, as described on page 35.

Another way to ensure good drainage is to improve the texture of the soil itself by adding amendments to it (also see page 35).

Channeling Excess Water

Often, you can improve the drainage in one area by channeling excess water to another place for disposal. To channel water below the surface, use drainage trenches containing gravel or flexible drainpipes.

Before you begin digging, check for the location of any underground utilities. You'll probably be able to dig a trench up to about 2 feet deep yourself. Anything deeper may have to be excavated by a pipeline contractor.

Use a trench shovel and pick for digging; a trench shovel will keep the sides of the trench straight and square.

Gravel-filled trenches. These trenches can catch and channel excess water running off hillsides, roofs, and concrete paving around swimming pools.

Dig the trench a foot deep and 6 to 12 inches wide, depending on the volume of water to be handled. Fill the trench with gravel or small stones. Unless the trench is part of your lawn, don't cover it with soil.

Flexible drainpipes. Flexible plastic drainpipes are easy to install and effectively carry runoff water away from the yard. Dig a trench about 4 inches wider than the drainpipe's diameter and at least a foot deep; slant it at least 3 inches for every 10 feet of trench.

Put coarse gravel or small stones 2 inches deep in the trench and lay flexible pipe on top, as shown above, at right. If you use perforated pipe, lay it with

the drain holes to the side so soil won't seep in and clog the pipe. Fill the trench with gravel. If it's part of the lawn, cover it with a layer of soil.

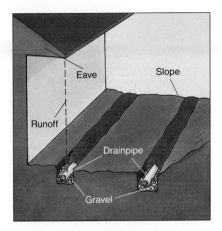

Flexible plastic drainpipes in gravel-filled trenches carry water away from lawn.

Collecting Excess Water

Drainage chimneys, dry wells, and catch basins aid drainage by gathering excess water and providing for its disposal.

Drainage chimneys let water pass through impervious soil layers to more fast-draining soil below. Dry wells allow water from drainpipes to settle slowly into the ground. The pipes from catch basins carry excess water to a disposal area, such as a storm drain.

Drainage chimneys. Use a posthole shovel or power posthole digger to dig 8- to 12-inch-wide holes spaced 2 to 4 feet apart down through poorly draining soil to gravel or sandy soil. Dig as many chimneys as you need. Fill each with small rocks or coarse gravel to let water pass through quickly.

Dry wells. Dig a 2- to 4-foot-wide hole 3 or more feet deep. (Keep the bottom of the hole above the water table.) Then dig trenches for drainpipes that will carry water into the dry well from other areas. Fill the dry well with coarse gravel or small rocks and cover with an impervious material, such as heavy roofing

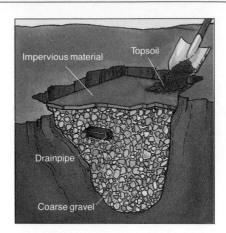

Dry well lets runoff water soak into fast-draining soil above water table.

paper; conceal with topsoil, as shown above.

Catch basins. To drain water from a low-lying area, dig a hole for a catch basin at the lowest point. Then dig a trench from the hole for a drainpipe that will carry the water to a disposal place, such as a storm drain.

Either set a ready-made concrete catch basin (available at building supply stores) into the hole and fill in with soil, or form and pour the concrete base and sides yourself. Set a grate on top.

Preparing the Soil

An understanding of your soil is perhaps the most important aspect of growing a healthy lawn. This knowledge will guide you in planting your lawn, as well as in watering and caring for it.

Once grass is established, you can aerate and fertilize it, but the actual soil base can't be reworked without a major renovation. Carefully prepared soil provides a strong foundation for your lawn.

Soil Types

Soil is a mass of mineral particles mixed with air, water, and living and dead organic matter. The size and form of the mineral particles, as well as their relative number, chiefly determine the structure of the soil.

Clay particles are the smallest mineral component, sand particles the largest, and silt an intermediate size. Clay and sand give their names to two soil types. A combination of clay, sand, and silt forms the basis for the soil referred to as loam.

Clay soils. Also called adobe, gumbo, or just "heavy" soils, clay soils are composed of microscopically small mineral particles. These tiny particles are flattened and fit closely together. Spaces between particles (for air and water) are also small. But because small clay particles offer the greatest surface area per volume of all soil types, clay soils can contain the greatest volume of nutrients.

When clay soils get wet, drainage—the downward movement of water—is slow. This means that loss of soluble nutrients by leaching also is slow. And because of its high density, clay soil is the slowest to warm in spring.

To test for a clay or claylike soil, pick up a handful of wet soil and shape it into a ball. Clay will feel slippery; when you let it go, it won't crumble (as shown below), and if you squeeze it, it will ooze through your fingers in ribbons.

Moist clay soil, *formed into a smooth ball, doesn't crumble when you let it go.*

Sandy soils. Sandy soils are the opposite of clay: particles are bigger and are rounded rather than flattened, allowing for larger pore spaces between particles than clay soils have. Consequently, sandy soils contain a lot of air, drain well, and warm quickly.

In a given volume of sandy soil, the surface area of particles is less than that in the same volume of clay. The volume of soluble and exchangeable nutrients in sandy soil is therefore correspondingly less. And because sandy soil drains quickly and hence leaches out nutrients faster than clay, plants need watering and fertilizing more often than those in clay soils.

If you squeeze a handful of moist sandy soil into a ball, it will form a cast but barely hold together.

Loam. Loam, a gardener's term for soil intermediate between clay and sand, contains a mixture of clay, sand, and silt particles. In addition, loam is well supplied with organic matter. Considered the ideal gardening soil, loam drains well (but doesn't dry too fast), leaches only moderately, and contains enough air for healthy root growth.

If you pick up a handful of loam, it will form a pliable ball that breaks apart with a gentle prod.

Soil Problems & Remedies

Although an amazing variety of soils support thriving lawns, many were not always so hospitable to the plants they now host.

The best way to determine what nutrients your soil needs is to run a soil test. This will tell you how much nitrogen, phosphorus, and potash you need to add to your soil, as well as its pH balance. Physical problems, such as shallow soil, will be visible to the naked eye.

Testing Your Soil

You can have a professional laboratory test your soil, or you can do it yourself with a home test kit (available at most lawn-care centers). Professional soil tests are more accurate and extensive, but they're also more expensive. To find a professional testing center, ask your County Cooperative Extension office.

Gather the soil to be tested from at least four different areas in your yard; dig to a depth of 4 to 5 inches. Mix the soil together before testing it or sending it to the laboratory.

Do-it-yourself kits are easy to use; they involve gathering soil samples and mixing them in test tubes with special solutions provided in the kit. Most kits come with a color chart against which you measure the color of the soil-solution mixture. Often, you'll have to estimate for shades between the colors shown on the color chart.

Chemical Problems

These conditions—acidity, alkalinity, and other related problems—are invisible to the gardener's eye but are revealed by poor plant performance.

Acid soil (pH 6.9 and lower) is most common in regions where rainfall is heavy; it's often associated with sandy soils and soils high in organic matter. Most plants grow well in mildly acid soil, but high-acid soil is inhospitable.

Add lime to such soils only if a soil test indicates that it's needed and only in the quantity recommended by a local expert. If you attempt to raise your soil's pH with lime, be sure that any fertilizers you use thereafter do not have an excessive acid reaction.

Alkaline soil (pH 7.1 and higher), common in regions with light rainfall, is high in calcium carbonate (lime) or certain other minerals, such as sodium. Many plants grow well in moderately alkaline soil; others will not thrive there because the alkalinity reduces availability of elements necessary for their growth.

If a soil test shows that your soil is highly alkaline, liberal additions of such organic amendments as peat moss, ground bark, or sawdust (see page 36) or fertilization with acid-type fertilizers

can help decrease alkalinity. For soil with a very high pH, use soil sulfur.

Salinity is an excess of salts in the soil. These salts may be naturally present in the soil, or they may come from water (especially softened water, which has a high sodium content), from fertilizers and chemical amendments, or from manures with high salt content.

Where these salts are not leached through the soil by heavy rainfall or deep irrigation, they reach high concentration in the root zone, inhibiting germination of seeds and stunting growth.

Periodic, thorough leaching of the soil with water will reduce its salt content. For leaching to work, drainage must be good. If the sodium content of your soil is particularly high, amend it with gypsum before leaching.

Chlorosis is a systemic condition in which newer grass growth turns yellow. The condition is usually caused by a deficiency of iron.

Iron deficiency is only occasionally the result of a lack of iron in the soil; more frequently, it's due to high alkalinity, poor drainage, or some other substance (usually lime) making the iron unavailable to the plant. To correct chlorosis, treat the soil with iron sulfate or iron chelate.

Nutrient deficiency may be the problem if the soil drains well, has ample water and the proper pH, yet still has failed to sustain plant growth well. It's most likely that nitrogen is missing from the soil. For information on combatting nutrient deficiency, see "Lawn Fertilizers," page 63.

Physical Problems

The most common physical soil problem is drainage. (Grading and more complex solutions for getting rid of excess water are described on pages 32–34.) But more often, poor soil conditions lie at the root of drainage problems.

Shallow soil (hardpan). A tight, impervious layer of soil, called hardpan,

can cause problems if it lies at or near the surface. Such a layer can be a natural formation or man-made, such as when builders spread excavated subsoil over the surface and then drive heavy trucks or bulldozers over it. If the subsoil has a clay content and is damp, it can take on a bricklike hardness when it dries.

A thin layer of topsoil may conceal hardpan, but roots cannot penetrate the hard layer, and water cannot drain through it. Grass will fail to grow, be stunted, or die.

Whatever the cause, time spent in correcting the problem at the outset will pay long-range dividends. The best method of dealing with a thick layer of hardpan is to scarify the soil, that is, rip it to a depth of about 18 inches with a chisel-toothed plow. This is work performed by a professional and only if the area is large and the problem severe.

If the hardpan layer is thin, you may be able to improve the soil by having it plowed to a depth of 12 inches or more.

Adding new soil. If you're adding soil to fill in low spots or raise the level of your lawn area, don't add it as a single layer on top of existing soil. Instead, add a portion of new soil (up to half, depending on projected new depth) and mix it thoroughly with existing soil by spading or rotary-tilling. Then add the remaining new soil to bring the level up to the desired height and mix it thoroughly into the previously tilled soil.

This extra work prevents the formation of an "interface"—a dividing-line barrier between two dissimilar soils that can slow or stop the downward movement of water.

If you purchase topsoil, try to find material that closely approximates your existing soil. Look for crumbly texture and avoid very fine-textured clays and silts. Try to steer clear of saline soils and soil that contains seeds of noxious weeds or residue from herbicides.

Amending the Soil

Adding organic or inorganic (mineral) amendments to your soil before plant-

A Selection of Organic Amendments

Organic or natural-material amendments, tilled into soil before planting, improve soil composition, resulting in healthy plant growth. Among popular choices are commercial compost, shown at left, which typically consists of sludge mixed with wood by-products; aged sawdust, in center, which won't steal nitrogen from soil the way raw sawdust does; and aged redwood sawdust, at right, the longest-lasting sawdust product.

ing improves soil quality, encouraging healthy root growth. (A soil test, as described on pages 34–35, will indicate which nutrients are present or needed.) Typically, an inch-thick layer of amendment (about 3 cubic yards per 1,000 square feet of soil) is added.

Organic Amendments

Vital to the fertility of all soils—and particularly needed in sand and clay—is organic matter, the decaying remains of once-living plants and animals.

Organic soil amendments immediately improve aeration and drainage of clay soils by acting as wedges between particles and particle aggregates. In sandy soil, organic amendments help hold water and dissolved nutrients in the pore spaces, so the soil will stay moist and hold dissolved nutrients longer.

As the organic matter decomposes, it releases nutrients, which add to soil fertility. But the nitrogen released by decaying matter isn't immediately available to plants. First, it must be converted by soil microorganisms (bacteria, fungi, and molds) into ammonia, then into nitrites, and finally into nitrates, which can be absorbed by the roots of the plants.

The microorganisms that do this converting are living entities themselves and need a certain amount of warmth, air, water, and nitrogen in order to live and carry on their functions. Soil amendments, by improving aeration and water penetration, also improve the efficiency of those organisms in making their nitrogen available.

The final product of the action by soil bacteria and other organisms on organic materials is the creation of humus. By binding minute clay particles into larger units, or "crumbs," this soft, sticky material improves aeration and drainage. And in sandy soil, humus remains in pore spaces and helps hold water and nutrients.

Types of organic amendments. Even the best of soils will benefit from the application of an organic amendment. Included among organic soil amendments are weed-free compost and manure, sawdust and wood shavings, ground bark, peat moss, leaf mold, and many other plant by-products, such as rice hulls and hay.

Several examples of organic amendments are shown above.

When you add organic amendments to your soil, be generous and mix them in deeply and uniformly. The mixing will add some air to the soil, and the amendments will help keep it there.

Cautions. The organisms that break down organic materials need nitrogen. If they cannot get all that they require from the organic material itself, they'll draw upon any available nitrogen in the soil, stealing the nitrogen vital to root growth; the result can be a temporary nitrogen depletion and reduced plant growth.

Most organic amendments either naturally contain enough nitrogen to satisfy the soil organisms or have been nitrogen fortified. But if you're using raw wood shavings or a similar noncomposted, low-nitrogen amendment, you'll need to add nitrogen.

After application, use 1 pound of ammonium sulfate for each 1-inch-deep layer of undecomposed organic material spread over 100 square feet. A year later, apply half as much ammonium sulfate, and in the third and fourth years, use a quarter as much.

Inorganic Amendments

Various inorganic soil amendments may be useful in special situations. But because they provide no nourishment for soil microorganisms, they're no substitute for organic amendments. Use inorganic materials only to supplement organic amendments when a specific need arises.

Included under inorganic amendments are lime and gypsum, both sold as fine powder or granules to be scattered over the soil surface and dug or tilled in. Although lime is the traditional remedy for raising the pH of overly acid soils, both lime and gypsum may improve some clay soils by causing the tiny clay particles to group together into larger "crumbs." This creates more space between particle aggregates, with a corresponding improvement in aeration and drainage.

Which material you use depends on the pH of your soil. Where soil is high in sodium, applications of gypsum will react with the sodium and clay particles to produce the larger soil "crumbs." If your soil is acid, lime will be useful.

Lime will add calcium to soil, and gypsum furnishes both calcium and sulfate; either material may be used as a nutrient supplement in soil deficient in those minerals.

Before using either lime or gypsum, check with your County Cooperative Extension office for advisability and guidelines.

Applying Amendments

Before you add any amendments, analyze the moisture content of the soil by picking up a handful and compressing it. If the soil crumbles to powder, it's too dry to work; soak it deeply, wait a few days for it to dry out, and test again. If the soil sticks together in a solid lump, it's too wet; in this case, wait for it to dry out and test it again. If it breaks apart into small clumps, it has the right moisture content and can be prepared.

If you're adding bulk amendments, use a shovel and wheelbarrow to make piles throughout the yard. Then rake them over the entire surface in an even layer 2 to 4 inches deep. Finally, evenly scatter fertilizer and, if necessary, a soil modifier such as lime or gypsum.

Although you can dig in soil amendments by hand using a sharp, square-edged spade, a power tiller (available at lawn-equipment rental outlets) is the tool of choice when you have a large area to cultivate.

Start by tilling in one direction; when you've tilled the entire area, make another run at right angles to the first direction. Dig up a spadeful of soil to see if the amendments are well combined. If necessary, till one or two more times to make certain the amendments and soil are thoroughly mixed.

Final Soil Preparation

Once you've completed the preliminary steps—grading, improving drainage, and amending the soil—you're ready for the installation of any underground watering system and for final grading.

Underground irrigation systems. When properly installed and operated, an in-ground irrigation system conserves water and is a far more efficient way to deliver water to your new lawn than is a hose-end sprinkler. You can have a professional install your system, or you can do it yourself. (For complete instructions, turn to pages 51–58.) No matter who does the work, it's most efficient to install the system just prior to the finish grading.

Finish grading. The goal of finish grading is to make the surface smooth enough for planting. After rough grading and tilling, the soil may be uneven, with shallow mounds and ruts in places. Use a leveler to smooth out the surface and make it even.

Finally, rake the soil, removing any debris, stones, or large clumps of soil the rake turns up. Then use the back side of the rake to smooth the surface of the soil and level it out.

Putting in Edgings

Edgings, whether made from wood, brick, or concrete, separate your lawn from other landscape elements and give a finished look to the areas they surround. They can even add decorative accents without distracting from the main focal point. Edgings are also helpful in keeping any surrounding ground cover or other plantings from invading your lawn, and vice versa.

Install lawn edgings after you've prepared the soil and re-established the rough grade.

A very practical edging you may want to consider is a mowing strip that separates the lawn from adjoining surfaces. The strip neatly contains the turf and also provides a surface for mower wheels so the blades can easily trim the edge of the grass. (For an example of a mowing strip, see the photograph on page 63.)

Mowing strips can be made from brick, poured concrete, or masonry blocks. Wood is the least-used material for mowing strips because it can be easily damaged by the mower.

Wood Edgings

Wood is a popular and easy material to use for edgings. It's best to use Construction Heart redwood or Select cedar, but remember that these labels don't always guarantee quality. Avoid redwood containing streaks of lighter sapwood, as well as cedar with large knots. Pressure-treated fir is another long-lasting alternative, but make sure the boards have been commercially treated.

For straight edgings, use solid 2-by lumber; for curves, use benderboard.

Solid-lumber edgings. Using a mason's line stretched tightly between stakes, dig a narrow trench deep enough so the top of the edging will be flush with the ground and any adjacent paving. To join boards for a long edge, either splice them with 2-foot lengths of 1 by 4s or 2 by 4s, or butt the boards at a stake and nail them when you set them in the trench.

Try to offset the splicing boards slightly so that they won't be visible on the part of the edging that shows above the ground.

Set the board on edge in the trench and drive 12-inch-long stakes (1 by 2s,

2 by 2s, or 1 by 3s) into the soil alongside the board, no more than 4 feet apart. The stakes should be slightly higher than the edging. (Place all the stakes on the side away from the lawn so they won't interfere with the use of an edging tool later on.)

Nail the stakes to the edging board, bracing the board from behind with a heavy hammer head or crowbar (this will also clinch the nails). To keep boards from splitting, blunt the nails or drill pilot holes.

Saw off the stakes at a 45° angle so the tip of each stake is level with the top of the edging board, as shown below, at left. Replace the soil and tamp it; it should be level with the top of the edging.

Benderboard. Perfect for gentle curves, benderboard is thin and flexible, usually ³⁄₈ inch thick by 4 inches wide. To determine the arc of your curve, use a homemade string compass, as shown in the inset below, marking the line with a sprinkling of agricultural lime.

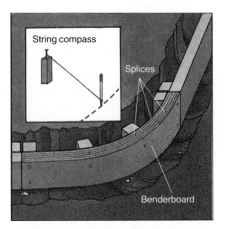

Layer benderboard to form curved edging; determine arc with a string compass (see inset).

Dig a narrow trench as described for solid-lumber edgings (see at left). Then drive in 12-inch-long stakes every 3 feet or so (the stakes should be slightly higher than the edging will be) to mark the inside of the curve.

Soak the benderboard in water, bend it around the stakes, and nail it in place, unless the stakes are on the lawn side of the edging. In that case, clamp the bend-

erboard to them instead of nailing, since you don't want stakes on the lawn side to stay in place permanently.

Bend additional boards around the outside of the first board, staggering any splices, until you've built up the curved edging to the same thickness as your straight edging. (If your inside stakes are just temporary, drive and nail stakes along the outside board.)

Don't try to force the benderboards into sharp curves—some boards will bend more easily than others, but a 6-foot radius is about as tight as you can get without breaking the boards.

Nail all thicknesses of boards together between stakes to keep them from warping or separating and pull out any temporary stakes on the inside of the curve. Saw off the stakes and fill the trench as described for solid-lumber edgings.

Masonry Edgings

Masonry makes a strong, permanent edging. You can install either a simple brick-in-soil edging or one made from concrete.

Brick-in-soil edgings. Very firm earth is required to hold these edgings in place.

To install, mark off and dig a narrow trench. Then simply place the bricks side by side, on end, in the trench. Use a bubble level to get the tops even. You can bury the bricks completely so their ends will be flush with your finished lawn. Or you can tilt the bricks at a 45° angle to give a sawtooth effect.

After the edging is set, pack soil tightly and firmly against the bricks.

Concrete edgings. Excellent for areas where your lawn borders a paved patio or driveway, these edgings are made from poured concrete.

To install such an edging, dig a trench and line the bottom with gravel. Around it, construct a temporary wood form that's your desired width and as high as the adjoining pavement. Pour concrete into the form and use a screed to level it. Cure the concrete for at least 3 days

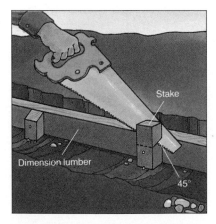

For solid-lumber edgings, saw off stakes at a 45° angle so tips are level with top of edging.

How to Read a Grass Seed Label

The label on a grass seed package is your key to choosing a high-quality seed. It can also help you avoid a product that could actually damage your lawn. A good sack of seeds is one that has your preferred seed type, a high percentage of germination, and a low percentage of crop seed, inert matter, and weed seed. There should be no noxious weed seed.

The label below, at right, describes a typical grass seed mixture. Here's how to interpret it.

Grass Seed Type

Grasses are separated into two basic groups, fine and coarse textured. Fine-textured grasses are bluegrass, fine fescue, Bermuda grass, perennial ryegrass, and bent grass. All other grasses, including tall fescue and annual ryegrass, are considered coarse textured.

Some gardeners prefer fine-textured grasses because they provide an esthetically pleasing lawn. If you want a fine-textured, picture-perfect lawn, look for a mixture in which fine-textured grasses account for more than 50 percent of the mix. (The mix percentage should be clearly marked on the label.) Whenever coarse-textured grass is included in a mix, it should be between 40 and 50 percent of the total; otherwise, your lawn will not have an even texture.

Cultivars will be stated; these varieties have been specially developed for color, texture, drought tolerance, or disease resistance and are usually an indication of quality.

Mix percentages. The seed mixture percentages listed on the label can be misleading. Remember that these percentages are according to weight—not number of seeds.

For example, there are about 230,000 annual ryegrass seeds per pound and about 2.2 million Kentucky bluegrass seeds per pound. Therefore, if the percentage on the label indicates the seed package holds 50 percent annual ryegrass and 50 percent Kentucky bluegrass, you'll actually be purchasing nearly 10 times more Kentucky bluegrass seed than annual ryegrass seed.

Germination. The germination percentage, listed with the seed type, must also be factored into the equation. The percentage of germination represents the portion of seed that will germinate under optimum conditions. To determine a seed sack's real seed mixture, multiply the germination percentage by the percent of the grass type.

Be aware that the older the seed, the lower the percentage of actual germination. Check the package for the "test" and "sell by" dates.

Other Ingredients

The items listed under this heading are potential trouble-makers. It's not always possible to keep these to a "zero" percentage, but in cases of crop seed, weed seed, and noxious weeds, try to get seed containers with as close to "zero" percentage as you can.

Crop seed. Usually listed first, crop legally is anything grown commercially by a farmer. Crop can be more of a problem in a lawn than weeds, since any chemical control you might use to kill certain crops could kill your grass, too. Crop can also include other turf grasses that might spoil the color or texture of your lawn.

Inert matter. This is simply filler, chaff, ground corn cobs, leaves, or even sand. It's generally harmless, but it should total no more than about 3 percent.

Weed seed. These are seeds from plants that don't belong in your yard. Again, the lower the percentage of weed seed, the better. Every grass seed package will contain a few weed seeds because of the harvesting techniques used in producing the seeds, but most of these weeds can't tolerate regular mowing and will be eradicated in a few months.

Noxious weeds. In most areas, it's illegal to sell seed that contains some noxious weeds—and for good reason. These can be highly invasive. Insist on a label that says "no noxious weeds."

A Typical Grass Seed Label

Fine-textured Grasses:	Origin	Germination
49.09% Pennant Perennial Ryegrass	Oregon	90%
24.68% Enjoy Chewings Fescue	Oregon	90%
24.41% Newport Kentucky Bluegrass	Oregon	85%
Coarse kinds: None		

Other Ingredients:

0.06% Other crop	1.73% Inert matter
0.03% Weed seed	No noxious weeds

by covering it with straw, burlap, or plastic sheeting to keep it moist.

Planting from Seed

Growing grass from seed not only provides you with the satisfaction of having started your lawn yourself, but also is much less expensive than laying sod. (For a comparison between seed and sod, see page 44.) Since the seed you plant will provide the foundation for your lawn in the years ahead, buy the highest-quality grass seed you can.

Choosing Grass Seed

The seed you select is crucial to the success of your new lawn. Your choice will depend on many factors, among them the availability of water, the proportion of sun and shade on your lawn, local climate conditions, and even how you plan to use your lawn.

Grasses are categorized as cool season or warm season. Most cool-season grasses can withstand winter cold, but many types languish during hot, dry summers. Warm-season grasses, on the other hand, grow vigorously during hot weather and go dormant in cool or cold weather. Note that many warm-season grasses are only grown from sod, sprigs, or plugs. Bahia and centipede grasses and many varieties of Bermuda are also available as seed.

Grass seed is sold straight, in a blend, or as a mixture. A straight is when only one species of grass is present. A combination of improved varieties of the same species is called a blend. When seeds have been combined from different grass species, it's called a mixture. To learn how to read a grass seed label, turn to page 39.

For information on the grasses that grow well in your locale, it's best to consult a local lawn expert. The three best sources are reputable garden centers, your County Cooperative Extension office, and professional landscapers. A comprehensive description of the most common turf grasses begins on page 19.

How Much Seed Do You Need?

The amount of seed you need for planting varies according to the type of grass you choose and your local environment. Read the seed container carefully—the amount of seeds per pound in various mixes and blends can vary considerably.

The label will often indicate how much area the seeds will cover on either a new lawn or an established one. Or it may tell you—usually in pounds of seed per 1,000 square feet of lawn—how many pounds are required.

Sowing Seed

The best time to plant grass seed in most areas is in the fall, early enough so that the grass has enough time to get established before having to face the rigors of cold weather. The next best time is the spring, after all chance of frost has passed and before the weather turns hot. Outlined below are the steps in the planting sequence. They're illustrated on the facing page.

Step 1: Seeding. Pick a windless day for sowing and sow seed as evenly as possible; a spreader or mechanical seeder will help. (If the seedbed is dry, irrigate and let the top inch of soil dry out before sowing any seeds.)

If you hand-scatter seeds, sow half of them as you walk across the area and the other half as you walk at right angles to the first route. Scatter the seeds at the rate that's recommended on the label of the package.

Step 2: Fertilizing. Using a mechanical spreader, apply a lawn fertilizer evenly over the surface of the new lawn, following the directions on the fertilizer bag. Don't use a fertilizer that's combined with a weed killer or weed preventer; otherwise, the grass seed will not grow.

Step 3: Raking. Use a steel rake to lightly scratch the seeds into the soil; don't stir the seed deeply, and don't try to cover every seed with soil. Then level the soil, if necessary.

Step 4: Mulching. If you expect hot, dry weather or drying winds, put down a thin, moisture-holding mulch, such as peat moss or screened, aged sawdust. To keep peat moss from blowing away (and to overcome its reluctance, when dry, to take up water), soak, knead, and pulverize it first. After mulching, roll the surface with an empty roller to press seed into contact with the soil.

Step 5: Watering. Water thoroughly, taking care not to wash out the seed, and then keep the seedbed moist with frequent but short irrigations until all the grass is sprouted. This may require watering 5 to 10 minutes each day (two or three times a day during warm periods) for up to 3 weeks.

You can use an underground watering system to do the job. Hand-sprinkling is difficult because you may have to walk on the new lawn; also, water distribution may be uneven.

Step 6: Mowing. Before mowing, check that your mower blades are sharp and the grass is dry enough so that the wheels of the mower will not tear the turf. For mowing instructions for a new lawn, see page 63.

Hydroseeding

This increasingly popular method of planting grass, a "one-step" operation, is now offered by most commercial landscaping companies. A selected combination of grass seed, fertilizer, and fiber mulch is mixed with water and shot through a hose onto your lawn. By applying all these elements at one time, hydroseeding can save you time and effort if you're planting a large area.

Hydroseeding costs more than planting from seed but less than planting sod. Like planting from seed, hydroseeding should be done in the fall or spring.

Seeding a New Lawn

Sow grass seed as evenly as possible over lawn area, using a broadcast spreader (as shown) or a mechanical seeder; or sow seeds by hand. Do not seed on a windy day.

After sowing grass seed, spread recommended lawn fertilizer over entire area, following directions on fertilizer bag. Be careful to apply fertilizer evenly.

Using a steel rake, lightly rake area, scratching grass seed into soil. Try not to disturb soil grade; if necessary, gently level surface.

Use a cage roller to spread a thin layer of mulch over surface to protect newly seeded lawn against effects of dry weather.

If soil has been mulched, roll entire area with an empty roller to press grass seed into contact with soil.

If you choose to have your lawn hydroseeded, make sure the company that does the job knows exactly what type of grass and fertilizer you want on your lawn. Both cool-season and warm-season grasses can be planted by hydroseeding, since both seeds and sprigs (see page 44) can be "shot" from the hydroseeder's hose.

Putting Down Sod

Laying sod allows you to perform landscaping magic. In just a few hours, you can convert bare soil into sparkling turf. Sodding is, essentially, the transplanting of living grass with some roots attached. The sod is rolled out on your prepared seedbed much like a carpet is rolled out on a bare floor.

Unlike seed lawns, a sod lawn can be installed almost any time of the year and will establish itself within 2 weeks. It's more expensive than sowing seeds, but it provides an instant green cover that's just as long-lasting as grass planted from seed. (For a comparison between seeding and sodding, see page 44.)

The relatively high cost of purchasing sod makes it important that you shop carefully for the right sod and the right grass variety. You also must determine how much sod you need and take care to install it correctly.

You can purchase sod through a nursery or directly from a sod grower. If you don't have a favorite nursery, look in the Yellow Pages under "Sod & Sodding Service."

Shopping for Sod

Whether you order directly from a sod farm or go through a nursery, find out how long the sod company has been in business. If the nursery has repeatedly ordered sod from the same company and has received no complaints, that's probably a good sign. Reputable sod producers guarantee the quality of their product and offer advice on how to plant and care for a new lawn.

Laying a Sod Lawn

Thoroughly incorporate amendments *into soil with a power tiller. Clean surface of any roots, weeds, or rocks. Then scatter fertilizer, roll, and level soil.*

Unfold sod strips *and lay them brick-bond fashion, pressing edges tightly together. Soil should be moist but not wet when strips are laid.*

Using a heavy, sharp knife, cut sod smoothly around sprinkler heads, along adjoining surfaces, and around trees or other obstructions.

Use a roller half-filled with water to press sod roots firmly against soil. Water every day (more often if weather is hot) for 6 weeks.

What to look for. One of the main differences between good and bad sod growers is weed and disease control. The good ones maintain very high standards in the field and supply sod that's virtually free of weeds and pests. Ask if the soil has been fumigated.

To check the quality of sod, unroll a few pieces. The sod should be moist, not dry or dripping wet. It's generally about an inch thick, but that can vary widely. Just make sure that it's an even thickness from one end to the other.

The sod should also be freshly cut. If you're in doubt, reach into the middle of a pile of sod. If the sod feels hot, it may not be suitable to use.

Pieces should be cleanly cut, not shaggy. They should be moist so they mesh readily when installed. You should also see root activity on the soil side.

Next, check the grass blades. They should be dense, like a dark green carpet, and be mowed to a uniform length. Poke around in the blades; if the sod is infested with grass weeds, you may find seed heads, even if it's been mowed short.

Plastic netting is used by some sod growers to reduce the time needed for a harvestable crop. Since it holds grass and soil together, netting also allows growers to cut sod thinner and so, they claim, root into your soil faster.

For home gardeners, netting may be a nuisance. Where the grass wears thin in shady areas or where the mower cuts too deeply, netting can become exposed, tangle mowers, or catch shoes. If you're using a sod with netting, make sure the soil is perfectly level before you plant. Otherwise, high spots will soon wear thin and expose the netting.

Choosing a variety. Depending on the supplier and your climate, you can choose from many kinds of turf. For information on the grass types that are available as sod, see the grass descriptions beginning on page 19.

Most suppliers offer purebred sods, which are strictly one type of grass. Although not as common as purebred sods, mixtures are also available.

Sod raised at a sod farm near your home usually has a better chance of doing well in your yard than sod from a different environment.

How much do you need? Determining the amount of sod you will need is simple. Just measure the size of your lawn to determine the square footage and buy that amount of sod, plus about 10 percent more to be on the safe side.

Sod generally comes in strips from 5 to 9 feet long. Each strip typically weighs about 30 pounds.

Ordering sod. Arrange to pick up sod or have it delivered the morning you intend to lay it. If the sod sits around too long, the grass starts to yellow and go shaggy. It will probably recover, but the lawn will be weak and slow to become established.

Laying Sod

Before you can install a sod lawn, the seedbed must be properly prepared (see pages 32–40). This work must be done in advance of purchasing the sod, because once the sod arrives at your home, it should be installed immediately.

The finished grade before installing sod should be 1 inch below the surrounding surfaces. The turf farm where you purchase the sod may recommend adding fertilizer before the sod is rolled out; the farm normally will provide the correct fertilizer.

The steps for laying sod are described below and are shown on pages 42–43.

Step 1: Soil preparation. After adding amendments and thoroughly working them into the soil, scatter fertilizer (if required), rolling it with a roller half-filled with water. Level soil again to 1 inch below surrounding surfaces.

Step 2: Laying strips. Starting along the longest straight edge, lay the sod strips brick-bond fashion on moist soil, pressing the edges tightly together. Walk on pieces of plywood, if necessary, to avoid disturbing the surface.

Step 3: Trimming sod. Use a heavy knife to cut sod around obstacles and along edges. Make sure cut edges fit snugly.

Step 4: Rolling. Roll the lawn with a roller half-filled with water to smooth rough spots and press roots firmly against the soil.

Step 5: Watering. Water daily (more often if the weather is hot) for 6 weeks.

Sprigging

Also called stolons or runners, sprigs are pieces of grass stem and root that are used to start lawns in place of seeds or sod. In fact, sprigging or sodding are the only methods of planting some grasses because they do not produce viable seed.

Warm-season grasses, such as hybrid Bermuda, St. Augustine, zoysia, and centipede, are most often planted by sprigging. Cool-season grasses, which include bent grasses, fescues, ryegrasses, and Kentucky bluegrass, aren't planted by this method.

It takes longer to establish a lawn by sprigging than it does by laying sod, but sprigging is considerably less expensive. Once a "sprig" lawn is established,

Seed Versus Sod

Before you begin the finish grading on your lawn, you'll need to decide whether you want to plant grass seed or roll out a carpet of sod. There are advantages and disadvantages to each planting method.

The pros and cons of seed. Although lawns grown from seed require more work to install and much more care to establish, they do have several advantages over sod. The principal advantage is that seeded lawns are much less expensive to plant.

The wide variety of seed that's available is another important advantage: it allows you to choose the grass or mixture of grasses that will do best in your own lawn.

Finally, because seeded lawns establish deep roots to anchor the turf, they're generally more durable than sod for heavy use and may last longer.

The pros and cons of sod. Ease of installation is probably the primary advantage of sod, but running a close second is the fact that such lawns don't require a lot of care to establish. You must water them, of course, but you don't need to fight weeds, seedling diseases, washouts, or birds as you do with seeded lawns. In fact, when you lay sod, you bury the weed seeds already in your soil, usually for good.

Another very persuasive argument for sod is that it covers the ground immediately, giving you a lush green lawn without your having to wait for seeds to sprout and take root. You get an instant reward for your effort and expense, and you don't need to worry about tracking dirt or mud into your house for several weeks, nor about seeds not germinating in certain spots.

In addition, you can plant a sod lawn in just about any season (except when the ground is frozen), unlike sowing seeds.

On the other hand, sod is much more expensive than seed and isn't available in as many varieties of grasses, so you may not be able to get the particular grass you want.

Also, because it introduces a layer of foreign soil, sod may not bond well to the soil beneath it. Sometimes, in fact, a sod lawn can fail to thrive.

it looks no different from a mature lawn started by sod, seed, or plugs.

Shopping for Sprigs

Sprigs most often come by the bushel, but you can also buy sod and carefully tear it apart and plant the runners.

The advantage of making your own sprigs from sod is that you can view the plants before making your purchase. The disadvantages are that this method takes time and effort, and sprigs can easily be damaged during the process.

It's usually best to purchase sprigs from a sod farm or from a reputable mail-order firm. The sprigs will be shipped to you in bags or cartons. It's very important to keep the sprigs cool and moist until planting time. Set unplanted sprigs in shady areas as you plant the others—sunlight can quickly damage sprigs, even if they're properly stored in containers.

Planting Sprigs

Sprigs can be short or long stemmed, but they must contain an intact root system, or at least two to four joints from which roots can develop. As in sowing seeds, care must be taken to plant sprigs at the right time, using the right methods and the right number of runners.

When to plant. Since sprigs come from warm-season grasses, the best time to plant is in early spring, after the danger of freezing weather is over. Warm weather provides the optimum growing conditions for those grasses.

How to plant. The fastest way to plant sprigs is to scatter them evenly by hand over the prepared seedbed and then roll with a cleated roller (usually available at nurseries that sell sprigs). If you can't find one, sprinkle a fine layer of topsoil over the sprigs. If you're planting a very large area, consider the method called hydroseeding (see page 40).

Another quick way to plant sprigs is to place them in the prepared soil and press down gently with a notched stick.

You can plant the sprigs individually, but this takes a great deal of time and is only advisable if your lawn is small. Placing sprigs 6 inches apart, make a small hole, put one end of a sprig in it, and press the soil back around it.

Fertilize the area and sprinkle the surface with water. Keep the area moist until the sprigs start growing.

How many to plant. The number of sprigs you need to plant per square foot of your lawn depends on the type of grass you're planting.

To establish hybrid Bermuda, hand-cast at the rate of 4 to 6 bushels per 1,000 square feet of lawn; plant St. Augustine, zoysia, and centipede grasses at the rate of 6 bushels per 1,000 square feet. If you're row-planting the runners, use about a third to half fewer sprigs than if you hand-cast.

Plugging

Like sprigging, plugging is a method of planting that allows grass runners to spread horizontally along the surface of the soil. Plugging is simply that—digging round or square holes into the lawn and inserting sod plugs.

Plugging is generally used only for warm-season grasses, such as centipede, St. Augustine, and zoysia. The plugs (2 to 3 inches across) are sold 18 to a tray, which will plant 50 square feet, and have an active root system that's ready to grow when placed in the soil.

If a plugged lawn is properly maintained, it will quickly fill in the rest of the lawn, providing a cover as lush and green as those started from seed, sod, or sprigs. Plant the plugs early, just before warming begins in the spring.

Buying Plugs

You can buy plugs by mail order, or you can buy sod and cut the plugs yourself. Nursery-grown plugs are cultivated under sterile conditions, ensuring that the plugs will be virtually free of pests and disease. Cutting the sod takes more time and may damage the grass, so it should be done with care.

Be sure the seedbed is prepared beforehand (see pages 32–40) so you can plant the plugs when they arrive. Although they won't wilt as fast as sprigs, plugs still need to be planted quickly. In the event of a delay, be sure to keep the plugs watered.

How to Plug

The soil should be moist but not wet before you begin plugging. You can cut holes with a shovel or spade, but it's much easier to use a round steel plugger or a plug auger suitable for use with a drill; look for these tools at equipment rental outlets. The pluggers make a clean, straight-sided hole that's the correct size and depth for the grass plug.

Cut the holes, spacing them as recommended for the type of grass you're using (generally 12 to 18 inches apart). Offset the rows checkerboard fashion. Remember: The closer the plugs are planted, the quicker your lawn will fill in.

If recommended, add a small amount of fertilizer to the holes before inserting the plugs. Plug-starter fertilizer has been specially formulated to provide quick growth of the plugs. The fertilizer has a small measuring container so that the correct amount is supplied to each plug.

Plant the plugs firmly, being sure that no air pockets are left around the plugs. The runners should be perfectly flush with the ground. Fertilize, if necessary, and scatter the soil removed from the hole around the plug. Water immediately. Continue watering on a daily basis for the first 2 weeks to prevent the plugs from drying out. Then you can water every other day for a month.

Once the plugs have rooted into the soil, begin mowing. The more the plugs are mowed, the more rapidly they'll spread. Always mow at the recommended height.

The plugs should be fertilized with a good granular fertilizer every 6 to 8 weeks until full coverage occurs.

Watering Your Lawn

Keeping a lawn lush, green, and healthy looking takes an understanding of your lawn's specific water needs—and an efficient watering system.

The first step is to become familiar with your microenvironment. Then you can decide on the best watering schedule for your lawn, as well as the most practical way of delivering that water.

Watering Guidelines

Perhaps the most common question asked by gardeners is "How often and how much should I water my lawn?" Unfortunately, there is no easy answer to this question. A general rule of thumb is to water infrequently but thoroughly. But because every lawn situation is different, you need to consider several site-specific factors—soil, microclimate, grade, and grass type—in order to determine your lawn's water requirements.

An understanding of those factors and the ability to "read" your lawn's water needs can eliminate much of the guesswork.

Your Microenvironment

When you apply water to soil, the water moves down through it by progressively wetting soil particles. As each particle acquires a film of water, any additional droplets move down to wet lower layers. Although water moves primarily downward, it also moves laterally (to a much lesser extent), particularly in claylike soils.

When you soak your soil, you're wetting each layer, as the water moves downward through it, to a condition known as field capacity. In this condition, each soil particle holds the maximum amount of water film it can against the pull of gravity; the amount of air space in the soil then is low.

As plant roots and evaporation draw water from the soil, the films of water become thinner, and there's more space for air. The film eventually becomes so thin that a plant will wilt. Field capacity depends on soil type, as explained below.

Other factors, as well, determine your lawn's watering needs, including your property's microclimate, its grade, and the type of grass you have. Because every lawn is different, each factor has to be considered independently.

Soil types. The three basic types of soil are clay, sand, and loam (to learn the differences and how to recognize each type, turn to page 34).

Each soil type interacts differently with water. Clay soil, with its fine particles, can hold more water than sandy soil which has fewer, coarser particles. Field capacity for loam falls somewhere between clay and sandy soils.

Because of its high holding capacity, clay soil can be watered less often than the other types. But when you do water, you'll have to sprinkle for a longer time and at a lower rate. An inch of water will

Providing the right amount of water at the right time helps ensure a healthy lawn.

47

penetrate only 4 to 5 inches in clay soil, while the same amount of water will penetrate 6 to 10 inches in loam and 12 inches through sandy soil.

In addition, clay soil absorbs water very slowly; for this reason, it must be irrigated slowly. Sandy soil, on the other hand, holds little water and dries out quickly; consequently, plants in sandy soil need supplemental water more often than they would if grown in another soil.

Loam falls in between the extremes of clay and sand. It has both large and small particles and will absorb and hold water moderately well.

Microclimate. Your watering schedule needs to reflect temperature changes, humidity levels, wind, and the amount of sun or shade on your property.

■ *Hot weather* causes plants to use water so rapidly that shallow-rooted ones sometimes cannot absorb water from the soil fast enough to prevent wilting. In such weather, you need to water more often than usual.

■ *Humid, cool weather* benefits lawns and allows you to water less frequently.

■ *Wind* robs your lawn of water in two ways. First, when you turn on a sprinkler on a windy day, much of the water may be carried away before it can penetrate the soil. Second, wind steals water that the plants draw up and release through their leaves. In still weather, the air around the leaf surface is humid, so the loss of moisture is not as great. Windy weather causes a more rapid water loss from leaves.

■ *Shaded lawns* need less water than unprotected lawns, unless grass is competing with tree roots for available water. If part of your lawn is constantly shaded while another section is in full sun, the two areas will require separate watering schedules. If you're designing an underground sprinkler system (see page 51), be sure to put the areas on separate circuits.

Grade. The steeper your lawn, the more often you'll have to water due to runoff. But water for shorter periods of time so the water has a chance to soak in.

Grass type. Grasses with deeper root systems generally require more water with each sprinkling to moisten the lower soil layers than grasses with shallower root systems. But you can water deep-rooted grasses less frequently, since the soil will lose moisture more slowly.

For information on the depth various grasses can send their roots under ideal conditions, see "Presenting the Grasses" beginning on page 17.

Watering Lawns— How Much & How Often

Recent studies have shown that home owners consistently apply at least twice as much water as their lawns actually need. Learning how and when to water can reduce your water bill substantially. It can also benefit your lawn.

Overwatering yields a shallow-rooted lawn and can leach fertilizers and nutrients out of the root zone. It causes grass to grow faster, so you have to mow more often, and can also encourage disease.

On the other hand, a little water wets only a little soil and won't dampen soil to any depth. This will produce a shallow root system and require you to water lightly each day during the growing season.

Tips for a More Water-efficient Lawn

Here are some good lawn practices that will help you conserve water.

■ *Water early in the morning.* Little moisture is lost to evaporation or wind, and the grass and soil will then be ready for the day's demand. Also, water pressure is usually highest at that time. Although night watering also keeps losses from evaporation to a minimum, it can create a moist habitat for pests and disease-causing organisms.

■ *Don't sprinkle during mid-day heat,* even if your lawn is showing signs of stress at that time.

■ *Plant a drought-tolerant grass* if you live in an arid climate or one prone to frequent droughts. For information on grasses, see the chapter beginning on page 17.

■ *Aerate your lawn* (see page 66) if you have a water runoff problem due to compacted or heavy clay soil. Or run sprinklers at full rate until runoff begins and then shut them off for about an hour to let the soil absorb some of the water. Repeat the process.

■ *With new lawns,* daily sprinkling is needed. In hot weather, it may be necessary to water twice daily to allow sod roots to grow or seeds to germinate.

■ *Dethatch your lawn* (see page 65) to allow water to penetrate into the soil more easily and reduce wasteful runoff.

■ *When mowing cool-season grasses,* set your mower higher than normal during dry times so that soil will stay moist for a longer time. Mow warm-season grasses at the highest recommended cut.

■ *Avoid overfertilizing* —it promotes more vigorous growth that will use more water. Don't fertilize your lawn unless it's showing signs of nutrient deficiency.

■ *Keep after weeds;* they compete with grass for whatever water is available.

Lawn Audit

*A **lawn audit** allows you to determine how much water your lawn is getting, and how evenly it's being watered.*

Generally, the most effective watering plan is to soak the soil deeply and not water again until the top inch or two begins to dry out. Watering deeply allows grass roots to extend deeper into the soil; although you'll have to apply more water to moisten the lower soil layers, you can water less often, since the soil will lose moisture more slowly.

Allow the soil to partially dry between waterings; this replenishes oxygen in the soil, necessary for healthy root growth.

The best way to find out about water penetration is to use a sampling tube, a device that removes cores of soil for close examination. You can also test water penetration by probing the soil with a thick piece of wire or a long screwdriver. Such a probe will usually move easily through moist soil but will stop when it reaches firmer, dry soil.

If the top inch or two of the soil is dry, it's time to water. Other signs of a thirsty lawn are grass blades that fold up, exposing their bottoms, and loss of resiliency (walk across your lawn—if your footprints remain for more than several seconds, you need to water).

In addition to these observations, there are several scientific methods you can turn to for help in determining a more precise watering schedule.

Using Evapotranspiration

The easiest way to determine if your lawn is getting enough water is to refer to local evapotranspiration (ET) measurements. ET, measured in inches or millimeters, is the amount of water that evaporates from the soil plus the amount that transpires through the leaves of the plant, in this case, grass. It's not easy to get a precise figure, but if you know how much water is leaving the soil, you can predict how much to replace.

ET figures vary from place to place, day to day, season to season, and year to year. But if you know the average for your general area and make adjustments to fit your lawn and the weather, you can water much more efficiently.

Many communities have guidelines based on ET figures to help gardeners determine how long to water. Rates are less in spring and fall than during the summer. To find out if there's an ET chart for your area, contact your County Cooperative Extension office.

In order to use the chart, you'll need to perform a lawn audit to find out how much water your lawn is getting from your present watering system. Even if an ET chart is unavailable, a lawn audit can tell you how uniformly your system is delivering water to your lawn.

Performing a lawn audit. Begin by placing a grid of equal-size containers or coffee cups around your lawn, as shown at left. Then run your watering system for 15 minutes. With the water off, measure the depth of the water that has accumulated in each container, keeping track on a piece of paper. (If you're using an ET chart, note the lowest amount and choose the water depth closest to that figure.)

If there's more than a ¼-inch difference between containers, you may want to make some changes in your system, whether it's adjusting or changing sprinkler heads or experimenting with the positioning of hose-end sprinklers. Once you've achieved a more consistent watering pattern, rerun the test.

Adjusting the figures. Although ET charts tend to recommend watering twice a week, more frequent, short sprinklings may be best in very hot, dry climates, in areas with very sandy soils, or for lawns that are very shallow rooted. Shorter sprinkling times, even if separated by only an hour, are also better where runoff is a problem.

Moisture Sensors & Probes

Both moisture sensors and soil probes can tell you when water is really necessary. Sensors, available in both automatic and manual versions, measure soil moisture pressure; a selection of sensors is shown on page 50.

Probes, which range from soil-coring tubes to an ordinary screwdriver, are less accurate than sensors but can still provide a good indication of how much water your soil is getting.

Moisture sensors. Moisture sensors gauge the moisture condition of the soil in a variety of ways. The type that measures moisture tension is called a tensiometer; it's a sealed, water-filled metal tube with a porous ceramic tip at one end and a pressure gauge at the other.

Other sensors measure temperature or the electrical conductivity of the soil. Your local nursery can help you figure out what the moisture content of your lawn should be.

Moisture Sensors

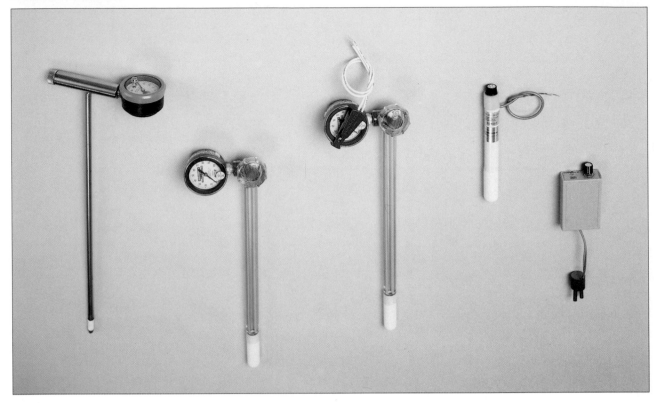

Moisture sensors include, from left, a portable sensor that goes anywhere; two permanent models, a manual one that can be used anywhere and an automatic one that's wired to a controller; and two electronic sensors.

Be sure to place the sensor in a representative area of lawn or in a spot that tends to dry out first. Also, its tip must be the approximate root depth of your grass.

Portable tensiometers, which are inserted into the grass, register moisture tension in about 5 minutes. These types can be used around trees and shrubs and in containers, as well as in lawns.

Manual or automatic tensiometers are generally intended for permanent placement. Use the manual kind if you don't have automatic sprinklers; check each time before you water.

The automatic version is designed to act as a master switch between your watering system's controller and valves; it allows watering only when the moisture level of the soil drops below a preset value. If you use this type, instead of scheduling an irrigation every 3 or 4 days, you need to set the controller to

water every day. The system will click on only when the moisture sensor tells it to.

Electronic models, designed for use only with automatic sprinkler systems, work in different ways. Some monitor soil moisture by combining two measurements—moisture pressure and temperature. Others gauge soil moisture by sensing the hydrogen charge of water in the soil.

Look for sensors at specialty irrigation stores and follow the manufacturer's directions for installation. Whatever kind you choose, check it often to be sure it's working properly.

Soil probes. Although they're less sophisticated than moisture sensors, soil probes can also tell you when to water, as well as let you see what's happening underground. Probes such as soil-coring tubes pull out a cross section of soil so you can see moisture content.

To help you determine if you're watering deeply enough, push a sampling tube into your lawn about 24 hours after watering. (You can't get a good core in mud or bone-dry soil.) If the core is moist only 2 inches deep and roots can grow 6 to 12 inches, you need to water three to six times as long.

Repeat the test in several areas of your lawn; then you'll know how long it takes for your irrigation system to wet soil to the desired depth.

The soil core can also help you tell when it's time to water again. If the core is damp, there's probably enough moisture. If the core is powder-dry more than a few inches deep, you probably need to water more often unless your lawn is very deep rooted and drought tolerant.

Soil-sampling tubes may be hard to find; check companies that sell scientific supplies or irrigation equipment for gardens.

For a quick test of your soil, poke a stiff wire or screwdriver into the soil in several places. If it penetrates easily for 6 or 7 inches, the soil has been properly saturated.

Underground Sprinkler Systems

The most efficient way to water your lawn is to use an underground sprinkler system. If you're putting in a new lawn or reseeding an existing one, consider installing such a system. You can also add a system to an existing landscape, but you'll have a lot of repair work to do on your lawn afterwards.

In most cases, you can install a system yourself; the basic steps—from planning to installation—are outlined in this section. Or you can have a landscaping expert do the work for you. For help in choosing a system or contractor, ask your neighbors for recommendations or look in the Yellow Pages under "Irrigation Systems & Equipment," "Landscape Contractors," or "Sprinklers—Garden & Lawn."

Even if you don't plan to do the work yourself, it's important to understand the basic components of a sprinkler system and the installation procedures so you can adequately operate the system once it's installed.

Basic Components

The parts you'll need to install a system include control valves, pipes and pipe fittings, risers, sprinkler heads, and a controller, or timer. The photo below shows how the components fit together to form an automatic system. For a manually operated system, you don't need control valves or a controller.

Assembling these components and installing them in your yard isn't difficult, but it can take time.

Control valves. These valves, the heart of the system, regulate the flow of water from your water source to the sprinkler heads. They're attached to the controller (see page 52), which automatically opens and shuts the valves.

Since there usually isn't enough water pressure in residential water lines to water the entire lawn at one time and service the house, too, irrigation systems are often separated into circuits. Each circuit is operated by a control valve that services a portion of the lawn or garden.

Circuits operate one at a time so the maximum flow rate isn't exceeded. They

Components of an Automatic Sprinkler System

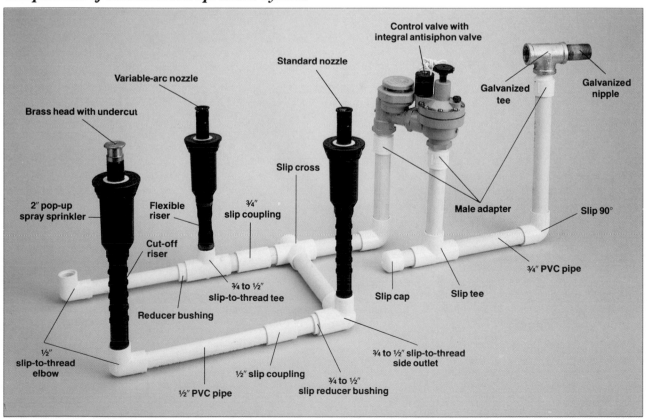

How to "Read" a Sprinkler Head

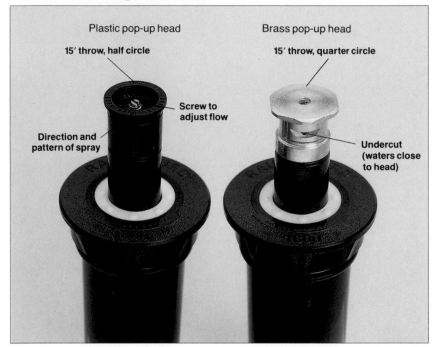

Plastic pop-up head
15' throw, half circle
Screw to adjust flow
Direction and pattern of spray

Brass pop-up head
15' throw, quarter circle
Undercut (waters close to head)

also allow for differences in the water requirements of the various areas in the landscape. (For more on designing circuits, see page 54.)

Each control valve should have an antisiphon valve, either integral or separate. Also known as vacuum breakers, antisiphon valves prevent the backflow of water into the main line.

Pipes. Most sprinkler systems use pipes made from polyvinyl chloride (PVC). In areas where the ground freezes, use copper pipe from your water meter to the control valves and PVC pipe for the rest of the system; just be sure to drain all water from the pipes before the first freeze.

PVC pipe comes in several strength designations. Choose heavy-duty pipe for areas where pressure is highest; use thinner, less expensive pipe for lines that are under no pressure.

Pipes in lengths of 10 and 20 feet with flared and standard ends are available. The standard end of one pipe fits into the flared end of the next pipe or into a fitting; a solvent is used to cement the ends together.

A general rule of thumb for sizing pipe is to choose a size that's the same as or larger than the house service line (usually ¾ or 1 inch in diameter). Manufacturers recommend a maximum of 13 gallons per minute (gpm) for ¾-inch pipe and 22 gpm for 1-inch pipe. (To calculate gpm, see the facing page.)

Pipe fittings. Available in a wide assortment of shapes, fittings, like those shown in the photo on page 51, allow you a great deal of flexibility when you're constructing the system. For example, fittings let you connect two pipes together at almost any angle; special fittings also allow you to connect PVC pipe to galvanized pipe and to connect pipes of different sizes together.

Some fittings screw together (always use pipe tape when screwing fittings and pipe together); others are cemented to the pipe with solvent.

Risers. Vertical pieces of pipe, risers connect underground pipe to sprinkler heads. Risers are designed to be used at different heights, depending on what's needed for each sprinkler head. Al-

though most risers are rigid, you can buy flexible risers that bend rather than break when hit.

Sprinkler heads. Manufacturers produce a large number of sprinkler heads in many different spray patterns, including full, half, and quarter circles, as well as rectangular shapes. Heads designed for shrubs, flower beds, and gardens, including drip emitters, are available.

Also on the market are low-precipitation-rate nozzles that reduce runoff, improve spray uniformity, and allow a larger area to be irrigated with a given amount of water. With matched-precipitation nozzles, available for almost every system, a sprinkler in a corner covering 90° of arc puts out a quarter as much as a 360° head—conserving water by allowing coordinated coverage.

The most common types of sprinkler heads used are pop-up heads made from plastic or, less commonly, brass (see at left); use these in open lawn areas where foot traffic and mowing will occur. Other heads are mounted on risers; use these where you need to throw water over shrubs or other plantings.

Some companies offer heads that are adjustable for patterns as well as for distance of throw.

Controllers. Most new controllers are solid state with electronic components (one type is shown on page 58). They offer features unavailable in the older mechanical timers. For example, dual- or multiple-program controllers let you water a lawn on a separate and more frequent schedule than ground covers, shrubs, and trees. You can also connect moisture sensors (see page 49) to such controllers.

The controller directs the watering cycle by automatically activating the control valves for the different circuits so they turn on for a selected period of time, at the hour and day you choose. The number of valves in your watering system determines the size controller you need.

If you think you may add more sprinklers or drip lines later, consider buying a controller with more station terminals than you currently need.

Because irrigation timers operate on low, 24-volt current, they're easy and safe to install. The wiring most often used is 18-gauge jacketed cable; if it's going to run underground, it should be labeled as being approved for burial.

Because each type has different operating instructions, be sure to follow the manufacturer's directions.

Planning Your System

Before you can buy parts and begin work, you'll need to prepare a fairly detailed map of your property that shows the location of all structures, underground utilities, paved areas, and plantings. You'll also need several measurements, such as your water pressure and the output of your service line.

This is a good time to discuss your project with an irrigation equipment retailer or landscape expert. Ask your retailer to provide you with a manufacturer's workbook, which can be helpful in drawing your map and describing the various components available.

Mapping Your Property

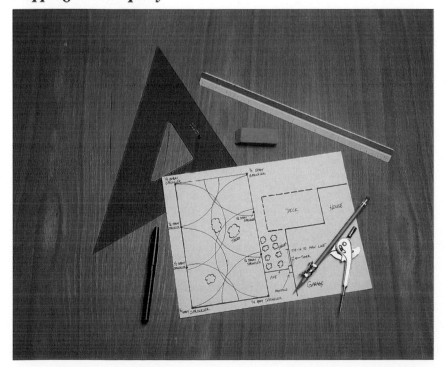

Mapping Your Property

The more detailed the sketch of your property and the information about your home's water system, the more confident you can be that the system you eventually buy will do the job you expect it to do.

Making a scale drawing. Using graph paper, plot the location of all structures, walkways and driveways, fences, trees, shrubs, lawns, flower and vegetable beds, and any other obstacles on your property. Be sure to mark where you intend to tap into the house's water supply (at a hose bibb, for example).

Now is the time to check with your local building department for any necessary permits. It's also a good idea to call your utility company if you suspect there may be utility lines buried underground on your property. Be sure to note those on your drawing.

Measuring water pressure. Most sprinklers will not operate efficiently if the water pressure (measured in pounds per square inch, or psi) of your water meter and service line is too low. A minimum of 20 psi is usually required. Your water pressure can be determined by using a pressure gauge (ask your irrigation equipment retailer to loan you one or check local hardware stores).

Measure water pressure at an outside faucet when no water is running in the house. Turn the faucet to be measured completely open. Record psi at each outside faucet location, taking several readings throughout the day, and use the lowest pressure.

If a gauge isn't available, call your water company and ask for the psi average in your neighborhood.

Determining gpm (gallons per minute). To make sure your main water line can handle the sprinkler system, you'll need to calculate the rate at which water travels through your pipes.

Ask your irrigation equipment retailer for help in measuring your main line's gpm. Or simply place a 1-gallon container under an outdoor faucet and count how many seconds it takes to fill the bucket completely. Then divide the total number of seconds into 60 to determine gpm. Write this figure on your plan; you'll use it when plotting circuits.

Note that to use this method of measuring gpm, the outdoor faucet must be the same diameter as your service line.

Plotting Your System

Planning your sprinkler system on paper will help you think the system through, guide you in ordering materials, and serve as a permanent record of where the pipes are buried (for an example, see at left).

You can design your own system or ask your retailer or other professional for help. Base your design on the various components offered by the manufacturer you choose.

Many in-ground sprinkler companies provide detailed planning and installation directions. If you haven't already chosen a manufacturer, ask for recommendations and choose carefully; you'll want to be sure the equipment is of good quality, the service provided is satisfactory, and the components will meet your needs.

Locating sprinkler heads. Make a copy of the scale drawing of your property and sketch in sprinklers in the corners and along the perimeter of your lawn. If you can't get full coverage with those heads, you'll have to place additional ones where needed. (Keep these to a minimum to avoid trenching in an existing lawn and to avoid locating heads in the mowing area.)

Using a pencil compass, draw the pattern needed for each head—quarter-circle heads in corners, half-circle heads along edges, and full-circle heads for center areas. On narrow or odd strips of lawn, use strip spray heads.

Then check the manufacturer's workbook for the radius, or throw, of each sprinkler head. Plan on a 100 percent overlap of spray patterns (spray should extend from sprinkler head to sprinkler head). Spacing the sprinklers too far apart will result in poor water distribution and create brown areas in your lawn.

Plotting circuits. Breaking your system into circuits, each directed by its own control valve, allows you to water lawns, gardens, and shrubs at different flow rates, durations, and times, ensuring that each area of the landscape will get only the water it needs.

The most important factor to remember when you're designing circuits is that the gpm of any one circuit cannot exceed the gpm from your main water line. To determine a circuit's total gpm, use the output chart in the manufacturer's workbook, writing the capacity of each sprinkler next to where it's located on your plan. Add up the figures for each circuit. Attach as many similar sprinklers on a circuit as you can without exceeding the gpm of your main water line.

Don't attempt to place different types of sprinkler heads on the same circuit. For example, standard lawn sprinklers must be on a different circuit from low-spray shrub sprinklers.

Group control valves into what's called a manifold to make operation more convenient and eliminate the need for extra trenching. It also makes it easier to attach the valves to the controller. The entire manifold can be buried underground, but it's a good idea to place an irrigation box around it for easy access. (See page 56 for more information on manifolds.)

Many systems have one manifold in the front yard and another in the backyard.

Where soil freezes, each circuit must be equipped with an automatic drain valve (install one at the low point of each circuit). The valves open automatically to let the pipes drain when the water is turned off.

Adding the piping. Starting at the control valve for each circuit, sketch in the piping that will connect the sprinklers on the same circuit. Try to avoid having pipes that run under driveways or other paved areas.

Assembling a shopping list. Using your drawing, determine the number of control valves you need, the number and lengths of pipes, and the number and types of pipe fittings and sprinkler heads. Know how many stations you'll need on your controller.

Tools you'll need for the actual installation work include a trench shovel and pick, PVC pipe cutters or a hacksaw

Installation Tools

Tools you'll need to install an underground system include, clockwise from left, a trench shovel, hacksaw, pipe wrench, pick, tape measure, string, mallet, stakes, utility knife, screwdriver, and pipe cutter.

for cutting pipe (pipe cutters are more efficient and don't leave burrs), a pipe wrench, and a sharp utility knife. (Those and other tools are illustrated on the facing page.) Have primer and solvent on hand for joining pipes and fittings.

Installation

Laying the pipe and building the manifold are two separate procedures that can be done in any order. Once those jobs are complete, you connect the manifold to the pipe and install the risers, sprinkler heads, and controller.

Working with Pipe

As you lay out your pipe lines, you'll doubtless have to cut and fit together sections of pipe. Here's how to do it (the steps are shown at right).

Carefully measure your pipe runs and cut the pipes with a pipe cutter or hacksaw, scraping off any burrs with a utility knife. (To prevent dirt from getting into pipes and to save wear and tear on your back, prop the pipe ends out of the trench when you work on them.)

When you join parts together, you must work quickly. The plastic solvent adheres quite rapidly—and once cemented, joints cannot be broken apart.

First, clean the area to be cemented with a cloth and apply primer to the outside of the standard pipe end and the inside of the flared end or fitting. Then brush solvent evenly over the primer. Place the pipes back in the trench and push the standard pipe end into the fitting or flared end and rotate it about a quarter turn. Hold the pieces together for about 20 seconds until set.

Wait at least an hour (longer in cold weather) before running water through the pipe.

Assembling the System

It doesn't matter whether you install your system from the farthest pipe and work toward the manifold or vice versa. But it is important to determine the

Working with PVC Pipe

Prop PVC pipes out of trench to make them more accessible; make sure ends are clean.

Brush primer on outside of standard pipe end and inside of flared end.

Working quickly, apply solvent evenly over primer coat.

Twist pipes a quarter turn and hold for about 20 seconds until set.

location of your manifold and the tie-in to the main water line before you begin digging.

The steps outlined below are illustrated on page 57.

Digging trenches. Although you can do this job by hand, it can be hard work; you may want to rent a trenching machine or hire someone to do the work for you. Lay out each trench with string and stakes and dig it at least 8 inches deep, using a sturdy trench shovel; use a pick where necessary.

To tunnel under sidewalks or other obstacles, attach a hose to a piece of galvanized pipe and turn on the water full force. The water will soften and tear away the soil. Once the soil is moistened, take the hose out and drive the

pipe through with a sledgehammer. When you're ready to push PVC pipe through the hole, tape the pipe's end with duct tape to keep out debris.

Tapping into the service line. Regardless of where you're tapping into the water line, be sure to turn off the main water supply to the house before beginning work. Three typical situations are illustrated on page 56.

To tap in at an outside faucet, remove the faucet and install a 1-inch galvanized or copper tee; then reattach the faucet. Attach a male adapter to the tee, install a shutoff valve, and run pipe from the valve to the manifold.

If you're tapping directly into the main line, cut out a small piece of the line and replace it with a compression tee. Then install a shutoff valve so you can turn off the water to the irrigation system and still have water to the house. (Some local codes also require you to install an antisiphon valve.)

Wait an hour for the solvent to dry; then flush out the pipe with water until it runs clear.

To tap in at a basement meter, cut into the service line just past the water meter. Install a compression tee and shutoff valve; then drill a hole through the basement wall above the foundation for the outgoing pipe. Be sure to install a drain cap at the lowest point of the system if you live in an area with freezing temperatures.

Assembling the manifold. The manifold, or grouping of control valves, can be assembled on your workbench or other convenient place. On the back of each control valve, screw in a tee fitting and attach a length of PVC pipe. This pipe will connect all your control valves (space the valves at least 3 inches apart for easy access).

Then attach separate fittings to the threaded outlet in the front of each control valve. Later, you'll connect the pipe leading directly to the sprinklers to these fittings.

Be sure to use fittings and pipe the same size as the valves. For future reference, write on the back of each valve the circuit the valve services. You can bury the manifold to keep it out of sight, but if you do, place a box around it for protection.

Laying pipe. Lay out the pipes as level as possible at the bottom of the trenches (some variation won't cause a problem) and make the required connections. If tree roots are in the way, either tunnel under them or cut through them with a saw or ax. Try to keep the inside of the pipes as free of dirt as possible.

Attaching the manifold. Connect the pipes to the manifold, being sure to twist the screw fitting hand-tight only. If you use a wrench, you risk stripping the threads inside the control valve. Also, use pipe tape.

Test the manifold for leaks; if there are any, unscrew the fitting, dry it off,

Three Ways to Tap into the Service Line

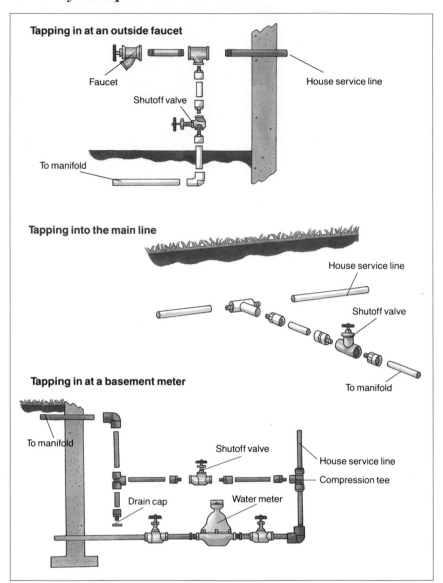

Tapping in at an outside faucet

Faucet

Shutoff valve

House service line

To manifold

Tapping into the main line

House service line

Shutoff valve

To manifold

Tapping in at a basement meter

To manifold

Shutoff valve

House service line

Compression tee

Drain cap

Water meter

and apply new pipe tape before handscrewing it back into the control valve.

Installing risers. With a tape measure, determine the desired height of each sprinkler head. The top of the pop-up sprinklers should be level with the finished soil. Cut a flexible riser to that length or use a precut riser.

Cut the trench pipe at each sprinkler location. Install a tee fitting and attach the riser, making sure that it's perpendicular to the surrounding terrain. This will ensure proper coverage.

Flushing the system. Don't wait until you've installed your sprinkler heads to flush the system, since dirt and dried solvent inside the pipes can rapidly clog the heads.

To flush your sprinkler system, turn on the water, one circuit at a time. (Make sure the pipe solvent has had at least an hour to dry before flushing, longer in cold temperatures.) You'll be able to see the water gush out of the risers. Wait until the water is clear before shutting it off and installing all of your sprinkler heads.

Installing an Automatic Sprinkler System

To excavate under paving, break up subsoil with a high-pressure hose; then drive a metal pipe through with a sledgehammer.

Shutoff valve allows you to turn off water to irrigation system and still have water inside your house.

Collected into a manifold, valves control flow of water to each circuit of your sprinkler system.

Measure carefully for risers before cutting them to ensure that sprinkler heads will be at desired height.

Flushing the system after attaching risers eliminates dirt and debris that would otherwise clog sprinkler heads.

Automatic tensiometer, buried in ground, activates controller when moisture in turf falls below a preset level.

Attaching the sprinkler heads. Screw the sprinkler heads to the risers, taking care to align them properly so they spray where you want them. If spray direction isn't clearly marked on the sprinkler head, check the manufacturer's workbook or ask your irrigation equipment retailer.

Installing the controller. Mount the controller (shown below) in your garage or another convenient, protected place near a power source. If there's some distance between your controller and the manifold, protect the wires by placing them inside a piece of pipe; bury the pipe in a trench, if necessary.

There are two wires on most control valves: one connects to a common terminal on the controller; the other connects sequentially to its own terminal. Once the wires are connected, set the watering controls (follow the manufacturer's instructions) and plug in the controller. Test the system by electronically opening and shutting each valve in sequence.

This is also the time to check for adequate coverage and attach any additional risers and sprinkler heads that may be needed.

Backfilling trenches. Replace the soil to a depth slightly lower than the original sod line. Flood the trenches with water to settle the soil; then add more soil, mounding it slightly. Sprinkle the mound for additional settling.

Maintenance & Repair

During the warm summer months, check your sprinklers at least once a month for broken or clogged heads. Look for leaks, poor spray patterns, or the resulting dry turf.

Cleaning clogged sprinkler heads. When a sprinkler is clogged, it will usually force water out at odd angles, or the spray will be greatly reduced. Try running a knife blade through the slit where the water is sprayed. If it doesn't clear, remove the head and clean it.

Replacing broken sprinklers and risers. With your hands or a wrench, lift off the broken sprinkler head and replace it with one of the same kind.

If a riser is broken and is difficult to extract, use a stub wrench. If solvent was used to install the riser, cut it off cleanly and attach an adaptor fitting and another riser.

Work carefully to avoid spilling soil into the line; if the surrounding soil is dry, wet it down first. If soil does enter the line, flush it out by removing all the sprinklers on the circuit and letting the water gush out of the risers.

Hoses & Sprinklers

Despite the increasing sophistication of automated sprinkler systems, nothing beats the garden hose for versatility. You can attach a variety of sprinklers to it, and you can move it almost anywhere you like. With a little care, a good garden hose will last several years. The trade-off, of course, is that garden hoses won't turn on by themselves at 4 A.M.

Hoses

The material a garden hose is made from determines the durability, flexibility, and weight of the hose, as well as how readily it kinks. When you're purchasing a hose, also consider its capacity (its inside diameter) and length.

Materials. Hoses are made from rubber, unreinforced vinyl, vinyl reinforced with fiber-cord netting, or reinforced rubber-vinyl.

■ *Rubber hoses,* which have a dull surface, are the heaviest and toughest of the hoses. Although flexible, they can kink, especially if left in the hot sun. However, they work well in cold temperatures and resist fire better than vinyl hoses (they're recommended in rural areas where wildfires are a danger).

■ *Unreinforced vinyl hoses* are smooth, shiny, lightweight, and inexpensive. However, they kink easily and can burst if the nozzle is shut off. They're also the least durable type, kinking badly in cold and hot weather. In freezing weather, an all-vinyl hose gets so brittle that it can easily break.

A Typical Controller

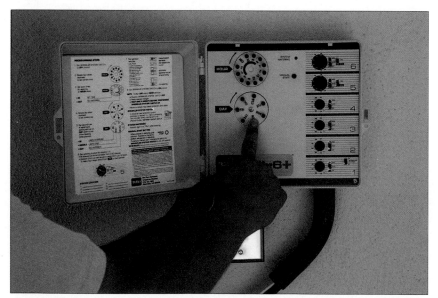

Hybrid controller *combines sophisticated solid-state circuitry with ease of use characteristic of older mechanical timers.*

■ *Reinforced vinyl hoses* have a textured, shiny exterior. Tough and kink-resistant, these hoses are also lightweight, so they're good choices if you need to move your hose frequently.

■ *Reinforced rubber-vinyl hoses* have a textured, somewhat shiny appearance. They're flexible, kink resistant, medium-heavy in weight, and durable.

Sizes. Commonly available hoses come in ½-inch, ⅝-inch, and ¾-inch inside diameters. (The outside diameter varies with the material used.) Threads are the same on each, so you can use the same nozzle with any size hose.

Although diameters differ by only a fraction of an inch, the volume of water each size hose can carry varies greatly. But there's a catch: using a nozzle or sprinkler minimizes the differences because these devices tend to equalize the amount of water coming out of the hose.

■ *A ½-inch hose* is lightweight and easy to carry and store. It's excellent for watering container plants; to water large trees and shrubs, choose a larger size.

■ *A ⅝-inch hose* is a good size for home gardens. It works well on larger areas even with low water pressure.

■ *A ¾-inch hose* is very heavy when filled with water but will deliver water at a faster rate than the smaller hoses.

Storing hoses. Hose hangers and reels not only make working with hoses easier, but they also help to preserve them by keeping them away from foot and car traffic. A hose hanger attaches to a wall—it's easy to wrap the hose around it in loops. Wall-hung and portable hose reels have handles you use to wrap the hose around the reel.

All types of hoses will last much longer if stored indoors during winter and kept out of the sun when not in use.

Hose-end Sprinklers

Many kinds of sprinklers are available on the market today, and each has its own sprinkler pattern, as shown at right.

Consider the size and shape of the area you want to water when shopping for a portable sprinkler. Here are some of the most popular types.

Impulse, or impact, sprinklers are popular because of their ability to cover large areas at a time. They also offer flexibility—they're easily adjusted to cover smaller areas. Their rotating heads send out a strong jet of water or a gentle mist.

Oscillating sprinklers sweep back and forth in a fan motion, applying water at a relatively slow rate. They're excellent for spot coverage, but they must be moved frequently for best results. Their pattern is similar to that of impulse sprinklers.

Revolving-arm sprinklers are useful but erratic. Most water falls from 4 to 8 feet out.

Cone sprayers, which force water out through holes, soak only a small area. For best results, turn the water down to half-pressure and move the sprinkler often.

Hose-end Sprinklers & Sprinkler Patterns

Impulse sprinkler

Oscillating sprinkler

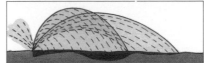

Revolving-arm sprinkler

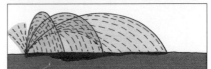

Cone sprayer

Lawn Maintenance

Government statisticians now rank lawn care as the number one leisure activity among home owners. You may sometimes wonder about the statisticians' choice of adjectives, but, if done properly and regularly, lawn maintenance can indeed be an enjoyable activity.

This chapter provides lawn-care information you can use with your turf maintenance schedule (see page 79). Reviewed are lawn mowers and mowing techniques, fertilizers, dethatching and aerating procedures, and techniques for renovating damaged lawns and dealing with lawn ailments.

Mowing

People have different ideas about what a well-groomed lawn should look like. But most would agree that lawns need to be mowed regularly to keep them looking their best.

Lawn Mowers

There are two types of mowers—reel and rotary. Reel mowers, usually five bladed, spin in a circular motion. However, they cut only in a forward motion and, unless powered, are practical only for small lawns.

Rotary mowers are usually tougher than reel mowers and can chop through leaves and twigs, as well as ride over rough terrain. They also cut forward and backward, which can be a definite advantage over reel mowers.

A word of caution: Although reel mowers are considered safer than rotary mowers, any motorized mower is potentially dangerous. Use with care and as directed by the manufacturer.

Reel Mowers

If you can cut your lawn in less than an hour and the terrain is not too hilly, consider buying a hand-pushed reel mower. Because it has no motor, it's less expensive and lasts longer than a motorized one. The only upkeep requirement is sharpening the blades. Moreover, a reel mower is usually much lighter and easier to handle.

Motorized reel mowers are very efficient and are favored for use on fine lawns and golf putting greens. However, they're often more expensive than rotary mowers and are suitable for use only on smooth, debris-free lawns.

Rotary Mowers

Push-type and self-propelled rotary mowers come with electric- or gas-driven engines. Electric mowers are usually quieter and less polluting than gas models, but the latter are more powerful. The popular mulching mower uses airflow to suspend clippings under its deck; the clippings are then recut more than a dozen times before falling, almost invisibly, into the turf below.

Fertilizers, such as this water-soluble type, provide essential nutrients to turf, ensuring healthy plant growth.

Hand-pushed rotary mowers. This type has been the most popular lawn mower for the past 20 years. The blades, powered by a small motor, spin parallel to the ground under a metal housing. You furnish the power to move it forward or backward.

These machines are usually very rugged—they can last a long time with a minimum of maintenance. However, they're relatively heavy and it takes some strength to push them. On a hilly or large lawn, you may want to consider another type of rotary mower.

Self-propelled rotary mowers. These are similar to the hand-pushed rotary machines, except they go forward under their own power. You simply walk behind and guide them. Most have variable speed adjustments. They're recommended for large lawns.

Ride-on mowers. For lawns of an acre or more, nothing beats a lawn tractor. These machines come with a variety of features, including a zero-turning radius that allows you to cut easily around trees, fences, and other obstacles.

Ride-on mowers can make mowing fun and easy. However, they're expensive, take up large storage areas, and require skilled maintenance and operation.

Purchasing a Mower

Savvy buyers match the mower with the job. Obviously, a gardener with a small urban lawn doesn't need to purchase a big, roaring ride-on mower. Conversely, a hand-pushed reel mower is going to make an endurance test out of cutting a 2-acre hillside lawn.

Here are some other purchasing tips.

Maneuverability. It's very important to be sure that you can easily handle the mower. You should be able to avoid obstacles with ease and get the whole job done without exhausting yourself. Also, keep in mind that you have to turn most mowers on their sides to sharpen the blades. If the mower is too heavy, you may end up putting off critical maintenance.

Starting systems. Yanking on a stubborn starting cord can be frustrating and can lead to arm and back injuries. Machines equipped with electric starters may be worth the extra cost.

The right handle. Make sure the handle of your walk-behind mower extends between your belt and rib cage. If more than one person is going to do the mowing, find a mower with an adjustable handle.

Using & Maintaining Your Mower

If you aren't mechanically inclined, you may want to consider a simple machine, such as a walk-behind with a 2-cycle engine that requires little maintenance. Or make arrangements with a local mower shop for regular motor tune-ups and to have the blades sharpened.

Winter storage. Before you put your mower away for the winter, check your owner's manual for instructions. Most call for draining the gas and oil, cleaning dried grass from the blade housing, and lubricating moving parts. Remember to disconnect the spark plug before you drain the gas. Once the gas is drained, reconnect the plug and run the engine until the gas in the line is used up. Empty the oil if required.

Just prior to the next growing season, add new oil, replace the spark plug, and clean or replace the fuel filter, if necessary.

Keeping mower blades sharp. Research has shown that lawns cut with a dull-bladed mower are more susceptible to disease and less attractive than ones mowed with a sharp-bladed mower. Mowers with dull blades will use about 22 percent more gasoline each growing season than mowers with sharp blades.

You can sharpen a rotary blade yourself. Remove the blade and sharpen it with a metal file. If heavy grinding is required, take the blade to a mower shop. Reel mowers require more precision sharpening; it's best to have a professional do the job.

Mowing Your Lawn

The rewards for mowing the lawn can extend beyond the nostalgic smell, look, and feel of newly cut grass. Mowing it at the proper height and at the right time can also help the lawn fight pests and diseases. Adjusting the height of the lawn can help it survive periods of drought or severe heat, while timely mowing can protect the fragile crowns from exposure.

When to Mow

Grass types and seasons will dictate how often you should mow. During their respective growing seasons, cool-season and warm-season grasses may require mowing every 2 or 3 days. However, off-season cutting may only be required every 2 weeks or even once a month. A good rule of thumb is not to rely on an established mowing schedule; instead, watch your grass and mow when it needs it.

Allowing your lawn to grow about a third taller than its recommended height before mowing will keep the grass greener and healthier. Letting it grow too tall will force you to cut too deeply into the crowns. This weakens the plants and gives weed seeds a better chance to germinate.

The height of the grass also affects the root system. If the lawn is cut to the correct height, the roots will grow deep and keep the lawn healthy. Scalping the lawn can shock the roots, either killing the plants or leaving them vulnerable to disease and other stresses.

Since grasses need a certain amount of leaf surface to stay healthy, the optimum height of each grass depends on whether it spreads vertically or horizontally. Horizontally spreading grasses, such as Bermuda grass and bent grass, should be cut shorter than vertically growing grasses, like tall fescue and Kentucky bluegrass.

For help in determining the ideal mowing height for your grass type, refer to the grass listings in the chapter beginning on page 17.

Mowing Techniques

If possible, change mowing directions every other time. Mower wheels can create ruts, and the grass may eventually grow lighter or darker in the rutted areas. Also, mowing in only one direction can create an unsightly grain—your lawn may begin to look striped or streaked.

If your lawn is too steep to mow up and down, try mowing at a slight diagonal.

Also, leave the grass clippings in the lawn. Clippings are 75 to 80 percent water and 3 to 6 percent nitrogen, ½ to 1 percent phosphorus, and 1 to 3 percent potassium—the same nutrients contained in most fertilizers. Calcium and other nutrients are also present.

If you don't let the grass get too tall between mowings, the clippings will be small enough to filter down to the soil. As clippings break down, they naturally fertilize the lawn. Lawns where clippings are removed require up to 2 extra pounds of nitrogen per 1,000 square feet per year. Wet clippings tend to clump together, so let your lawn dry before cutting.

Mowing New Lawns

Since the root systems of new lawns are not yet firmly established, go easy on the first couple of mowings. Mow slowly, especially around corners, so the wheels don't tear up the grass. Never cut the grass when it's wet. Let it dry and then water right after mowing.

Be sure not to mow too low: it's better to leave the new grass too high than to risk scalping it. However, when the lawn has grown a third taller than its optimum height, don't be afraid to cut it. Mowing helps the plants spread, and the clippings provide a good natural fertilizer.

Trimming & Edging

Regardless of the mower you use, you'll probably have some trimming and edging to do along sidewalks and driveways,

walls, trees, fences, and beds, unless you have a mowing strip, as shown below. On small lawns, hand shears or clippers will usually do the job, but on larger lawns hand-held motorized trimmers and edgers are quicker and easier.

Trimmers. Powered by gasoline or electricity, nylon string trimmers stand midway between mowers and edgers. Nylon filaments are attached to a quickly rotating disk mounted at an angle at the end of a long handle; the spinning filaments cut tall grass and weeds with a whipping action. Watch out for flying debris and avoid hitting the trunks of young trees with the trimmer wire.

Gas-powered trimmers that feature reciprocating blades reduce the danger of flying debris. They're lightweight and maneuverable, and their blades stop immediately when the engine is shut off.

Edgers. If your lawn is small and there's little edging to be done, an inexpensive manually operated edger may be all you need. But if you have a number of edges to cut, you may want to consider any of a variety of cordless electric or gas-powered edgers now available.

Most basic of these tools are the various short-handled shears. One type operates by vertical squeezing action: one handle is above the other, and each squeeze closes the blades, which cut as they pass by one another. In another model, one blade remains in a fixed position while the other blade slices across it: the harder you squeeze on the handles, the more tension you apply to the blades. Still another kind operates by horizontal action.

Long-handled, heavy-duty grass shears let you stand up to cut lawn edges and the margins of thick ground covers. They'll even cut right into the sod. Also available are grass shears with wheels at the base of a 3-foot handle. As you wheel it along, you squeeze a handle operating scissors-action blades that cut the grass.

Lawn Fertilizers

Experts don't always agree about the type and amount of fertilizer each lawn needs, but they do agree on one thing—most lawns require it. Lawns are unnatural environments where plants are crowded together. Therefore, they require higher amounts of nutrients than are available naturally. This is especially

Mowing along a Mowing Strip

Wheels of rotary mower *ride on a concrete mowing strip, which allows mower to trim grass closely along edge of lawn.*

true on lawns where the clippings, a natural fertilizer, are removed after mowing.

Some fertilizers now come mixed with pesticides. Choosing the right mixture and applying it correctly can save you time and money by allowing you to do two jobs in one. Remember—nearly all fertilizers require a thorough watering after application. If left dry, most fertilizers will burn the lawn.

Understanding Fertilizers

Grasses need about 16 different mineral elements to survive. Most of these are available naturally in the soil. However, three primary elements—nitrogen, phosphorus, and potassium—must be added regularly in the form of a fertilizer.

Nitrogen is the key to healthy lawns, since it stimulates leaf growth. Phosphorus is needed for strong root growth, and potassium helps with internal plant development and functions.

Before you choose a fertilizer, you need to test your soil to see which nutrients it needs (see page 34). Home test kits are available at most lawn-care stores. However, results from these kits can be difficult to interpret. If you have questions, you can have your soil checked at a private lab (ask your County Cooperative Extension office for names). Once you know what your lawn needs, you can buy the correct fertilizer.

Regardless of the brand you choose, the package label should contain three numbers, such as 26-3-3, 6-4-2, or 10-10-0. The first number, the most important, refers to the percentage of nitrogen present. The second number refers to phosphorus and the third to potassium. If one of the numbers is zero, that element isn't included.

Choosing a Fertilizer

A bewildering selection of fertilizers is available, including granular types packaged in cartons and sacks, and liquid ones in bottles. In addition, you'll find both organic and synthetic fertilizers, as well as combination products.

Dry granular fertilizers. Most fertilizers sold are in dry form. You sprinkle or spread them onto a lawn and then scratch, rake, or dig them into the soil; or you can apply them in subsurface strips. When the ground is watered, the granules dissolve, beginning their fertilizing action quickly. Depending on the type of nitrogen in the fertilizer, they can last up to several months.

Controlled-release fertilizers are balls of complete fertilizers coated with a permeable substance. When moistened, a small amount of nutrients leaches through the coating until the encapsulated fertilizer is used up. These products last from 3 to 8 months.

Liquid fertilizers. Liquid fertilizers are easy to use, avoid the risk of burning the lawn (as long as you follow label directions for dilution), and are immediately available to roots. However, they're less practical than dry types for large lawns because they are more expensive, are harder to apply evenly, and must be used more often since small amounts of nutrients are applied each time.

Available in a variety of formulas, all liquid fertilizers must be used with water: some are concentrated solutions you dilute in water; others are dry concentrates you dissolve in water.

Organic fertilizers. The word "organic" simply means that the nutrients contained in the product are derived solely from the remains or from a by-product of a once-living organism. Cottonseed meal, blood meal, bone meal, hoof-and-horn meal, and manures are examples of organic fertilizers. (Urea is a synthetic organic fertilizer—an organiclike substance manufactured from inorganic materials.)

Most of these products packaged as fertilizers will be labeled with their nitrogen-phosphate-potassium ratios. Usually, an organic fertilizer is high in just one of the three major nutrients and low in the other two, although some are chemically fortified with the other nutrients.

In general, the organics release their nutrients over a fairly long period. However, they may not release enough of their principal nutrient at the time when the plant needs it for best growth. Because they depend on soil organisms to release the nutrients, most organic fertilizers are effective only when soil is moist and warm enough for the organisms to be active.

Although manure is a complete organic fertilizer, it may be low in some important nutrients. Manures are best used as mulches or soil conditioners.

Synthetic fertilizers. These manufactured fertilizers release their nutrients into the soil quickly and turn grass greener shortly after application. However, the results are temporary unless fertilizer is applied often during the growing season. Synthetic fertilizers can easily burn a lawn, so caution must be used when they're applied.

Combination products. You can buy fertilizers combined with insecticides, weed killers, fungicides, or moss killers. These products are appropriate if you need the extra ingredient every time you fertilize; if not, it's more economical to buy it separately.

When to Fertilize

Fertilizing needs vary with grass type, climate, and the type of fertilizer used. Each fertilizer is labeled with application instructions, but you should also learn to "read" your own lawn so you can recognize when it requires fertilizer. Loss of color is one obvious sign; another is lack of vigor.

Usually, it's necessary to fertilize once or twice in the spring as the growing season begins. If you're using fast-release fertilizer, more frequent applications will be necessary. Many lawns, especially those in warm-climate areas, also require additional fertilization in the fall. Summer applications are risky in most areas, since high temperatures can easily cause a lawn to burn.

For guidelines on how much fertilizer to use on your lawn, see the grass

Fertilizing with a Drop-spreader

Drop-spreader *allows for even distribution of fertilizer; make two passes, one perpendicular to the other, using half the fertilizer during each pass.*

listings beginning on page 19. If you're still in doubt as to when to fertilize, consult a local lawn professional.

Fertilizing Techniques

The three common methods of applying fertilizer are hand-casting, using an applicator, and spraying water-soluble fertilizers through a hose. Regardless of the method you choose, be sure to use the right amount of fertilizer and spread it evenly.

Hand-casting. You can use this method with any type of solid fertilizer. However, it's safest with organic fertilizers, since there's less danger of grass burn.

Hand-cast the fertilizer across the lawn in one direction, applying it at full strength. Then repeat at a 90° angle, using only half as much fertilizer. If you think you've put too much on one area, use a rake to spread it out.

Using an applicator. Hand-operated broadcasters and walk-behind broadcasters and drop-spreaders are commonly used to apply dry fertilizer.

■ *Hand-operated broadcasters* come in different shapes and sizes. A hand crank activates a small hopper that throws the fertilizer out in all directions (one type is shown on page 41).

Start at one end of your lawn and make a run. Then pace off the swath diameter and make your next run parallel to the first. It's best to overlap by about a third. To avoid overfertilizing, stop turning the hand crank as you make your turn at the end of your run.

Be sure to fill the applicator over a driveway or sidewalk so spillage does not burn a patch in the lawn.

■ *Walk-behind broadcasters,* like the one shown on page 67, are pushed from behind like lawn mowers. More accurate than hand-operated broadcasters, they're also more expensive. They're ideal for larger lawns and apply fertilizer evenly. Overlap slightly as you make your runs to avoid creating wheel depressions.

■ *Walk-behind drop-spreaders,* like the one shown above, drop the fertilizer straight down into the turf instead of throwing it out like broadcast spreaders. Therefore, it takes longer to fertilize a yard using a drop-spreader, but they're

the most accurate of all fertilizing applicators.

You can rent this type of applicator; have the rental operator show you how to calibrate how much fertilizer the drop-spreader will apply at one time.

Spraying fertilizers. Water-soluble fertilizers are easily applied using a hose-end sprayer. The fertilizer container should provide a chart showing the water-to-fertilizer mixing ratio.

Divide the lawn in half with a rope or sticks and spray evenly. Try to reach the halfway point in the lawn when the hose container reaches half-empty. Work carefully and quickly so you finish the rest of the lawn as the container empties.

Dethatching & Aeration

When nutrients, water, and air are unable to penetrate the soil because of thatch buildup or soil compaction, bare spots may begin to appear, and grass will no longer thrive. Dethatching and aerating are two practices that can restore your lawn to health.

Dethatching

Thatch is the layer of stems, stolons, rhizomes, roots, and debris that accumulates between the surface of the soil and the green grass blades above. It's a perfect hideout for insects and prevents water from reaching the soil.

Controlling thatch is one of the most important and overlooked steps in lawn care. Almost every lawn needs dethatching at least once a year. Water and fertilizers are absorbed much more quickly when thatch is cleared away, and diseases and insects have a tougher time getting established. Also, grass seeds germinate more quickly, roots grow deeper, and the lawn remains a deep green longer in the fall and regains its color earlier in the spring.

Some grasses are more susceptible to thatch buildup than others. The creeping grasses, most notably Bermuda grass, St. Augustine grass, bent grass, zoysia grass, and Kentucky bluegrass, develop thatch quickly. A lawn planted with one of those grasses will have to be dethatched more often than a lawn planted with a different grass.

When to Dethatch

Lawn experts recommend dethatching your lawn when the thatch depth has reached ½ inch. To check the depth, cut a 2-inch–square piece of lawn, 3 inches deep, remove it from the soil, and measure the thickness of the thatch (the distance from the top of the brown thatch layer to the top of the soil).

Another indication that your lawn needs dethatching is when your mower leaves brown streaks and patches in the lawn. This occurs where the thatch is soft and the mower wheels sink in, allowing the blades to scalp the grass.

When you dethatch also depends on your climate and the type of grass you have. Autumn is preferable for cool-season grasses; plan to dethatch early enough in the season so there's still at least a month of good growing weather during which the grass can recuperate. Cool-season grasses can be dethatched in early spring also.

The best time to dethatch warm-season grasses is late spring, when they can recover quickly.

How to Dethatch

The most efficient way to dethatch your lawn—and the proper way—is to use a dethatching machine, often referred to as a vertical cutter. Dethatching machines look like lawn mowers, but they slice the turf vertically with knifelike scissors, tearing through thatch layers and low grass runners.

Since the calibration of the depth and width of the cutter blades is critical, you may want to hire a professional to do the dethatching. Contact a local lawn-care service company.

If you prefer to do the work your-self, rent a vertical cutter from a local equipment rental company (dethatching a 1,000-square-foot lawn will usually take one person a little more than 2 hours). Note that although the machine is small enough to fit into the trunk of most cars, it is very heavy.

The key to proper dethatching is correct adjustment of the vertical cutter blades. For tough warm-season grasses like Bermuda grass, the cutter blades should be set to slice completely through the thatch layer and about an inch into the soil. To promote heavy thinning, set the blades about an inch apart.

For more fragile grass types, the blades should be set higher and about 3 inches apart. Check with your local lawn-care center for recommended settings. Most rental companies will help you make the blade settings.

When cutting, make several criss-crossing passes to lift and loosen the tough, interlocking runners that hold thatch.

The soil should be damp but not wet when you use a dethatcher. Don't let the loose thatch material remain on the surface of your lawn. Instead, rake it up and dispose of it properly.

Aeration

Lawns grown in clay soils or those subjected to heavy foot traffic can easily become compacted. Aeration is simply a method of punching holes into the turf to allow moisture, oxygen, and nutrients to penetrate the soil. It can also help break up thatch, which discourages water absorption and root growth.

When to aerate. The timing and frequency of aeration depend on your soil type. Clay soils compact easily and must be aerated often, generally at least twice a year. Sandy soils need aerating only about once a year. Since aeration schedules are site and soil specific, check with a local lawn-care professional before developing your own schedule.

How to aerate. To aerate your lawn, you can use either a motorized aerating machine or a foot-press aerator that you push into the soil, much like a shovel. (Either tool can be rented from an equipment rental company.) Many professional lawn-care companies also provide aerating service.

Although motorized aerators are more expensive to rent, they're quicker, easier, and usually much more efficient to use than the foot-press types. Whichever tool you choose, aeration holes should penetrate 2 to 4 inches into the soil. Most lawns require a single coverage, but if you have clay soil or if your lawn hasn't been aerated for more than a year, do it twice, the second time at a 90° angle to the first pass.

Back-comb the soil with a rake to level it; or you can break up the turf cores by dragging a metal mat over them and then using them to fill in low spots in the lawn.

Lawn Renovation

Although lawns can have a lengthy life span, there are times when an entire lawn—or a substantial portion of it—must be replanted. When bare spots aren't responding to your normal cultural practices, it's time to renovate.

Renovations aren't difficult and don't require a lot of time, but they can make a big difference in how your lawn looks. Before beginning any work, apply a translocating nonselective herbicide to the lawn to kill all grasses and weeds (follow the manufacturer's directions for use). Wait until the chemical has had enough time to do its work before you proceed.

The steps in the renovation process are outlined below. See the facing page for a look at the process.

Step 1: Dethatching. Use a dethatching machine, available at most equipment rental companies, to slice through the dead grass to allow the seeds, water, and fertilizer access to the soil. The dethatching blades leave slits in the soil that will be filled with new seed after the area is raked and leveled.

Six Steps in a Lawn Renovation

Before renovation, *lawn looks blotchy and unhealthy. Numerous bare spots mark surface.*

Dethatching machine, *or vertical cutter, tears through thatch layers and slices into soil.*

Rake up old grass *and cart it off to a disposal site. (Thatch is not suitable to use as mulch or compost.)*

Power aerator *pulls up turf cores, reducing compaction and permitting water, seed, and air to penetrate soil more easily.*

Walk-behind broadcast spreader, *ideal for large lawn areas, throws grass seed out evenly.*

Apply fertilizer *and, if desired, rake lightly to scratch grass seeds into soil. Water, keeping soil moist at all times.*

On very small lawns, you can dethatch by mowing close to the ground and using a metal rake to tear up the thatch. For detailed instructions on dethatching, see page 65.

Step 2: Raking. Use a rake to gather up the old grass and weeds, thereby eliminating unwanted seeds that will compete with the new ones you'll plant. Then rake the area level.

Because thatch decomposes very slowly, it's not a good idea to use it either as mulch or as part of a compost pile.

Step 3: Aeration. Punching holes in the turf, a process known as aeration (see page 66), allows moisture, fertilizer, grass seed, and air to penetrate the soil. Using a power or foot-press aerator, cover the entire area to be renovated.

The aerator pulls plugs of soil, called turf cores, out of your lawn, easing soil compaction and giving the new lawn roots room to grow.

Step 4: Seeding. Put down grass seed or start your lawn with sprigs or plugs. If you're laying sod instead, you may need to test the soil and add any necessary soil amendments. (For help, see the chapter beginning on page 29.)

Step 5: Fertilizing. Apply fertilizer as described on page 65, following the manufacturer's directions.

Step 6: Watering. The lawn must be kept moist at all times. If you're renovating during a summer hot spell, it may be necessary to sprinkle the seed bed several times a day. Once the new grass has grown a third taller than its optimum height, you can mow it. Be careful not to cut it too closely.

Weeds, Pests & Diseases

Although on the surface lawns appear to be peaceful, soft mats to walk on, under the blades a daily battle takes place. Militant weeds, insects, and grass-destroying diseases are constantly attacking your lawn. They'll take advantage of any turf weakness caused by improper watering, too much thatch, soil nutrient depletion, or compaction of soil.

Waging War Against Weeds

Technically, weeds are annual or perennial plants that grow where they're unwanted. Weed seed comes in all packages of lawn seed; it can also be blown in by wind, washed in by water runoff, or carried in by animals and humans.

Types of Weeds

Weeds are classified into two groups: grassy and broad leaved. For a close look at some common grassy and broad-leaved weeds and information on how to control them, see the chart beginning on page 70.

Grassy weeds. Any grass unwanted by the gardener is considered a grassy weed. The most common is hairy crabgrass. Although it's not always the culprit (many other weeds are mistaken for hairy crabgrass), it remains king of the grassy weeds.

Hairy crabgrass seedlings grow 2 to 4 leaves that form large, flat, stem-rooting clumps during summer. The weed looks like a large, green, upside-down spider at maturity, and it spreads very quickly. Other common grassy weeds are Bermuda grass, dallis grass, and quack grass.

Broad-leaved weeds. All nongrassy plants that invade your lawn are considered broad-leaved weeds. Spurge, dandelion, and chickweed are common examples.

Eradicating Weeds

Getting rid of weeds isn't usually a difficult job if weeds are kept to a minimum by such good lawn practices as frequent mowing, watering, and fertilizing. Weeding can be done by hand or with chemical herbicides. Some biological products, such as herbicidal soaps, are also helpful if the infestation is not too extensive.

Since herbicides contain toxic materials, they should always be used with caution. Be sure to read labels carefully and follow directions exactly.

Weeding by hand. Pull annual weeds out by hand, if possible, or use a weeding tool; it's important to pull out the roots as well as the tops. Although hand-pulling weeds takes time and effort, it does ensure that the weed is totally removed; it also avoids the use of chemical herbicides.

Using herbicides. If used incorrectly, herbicides can injure or kill desirable turf and commit unwanted poisons into the environment. Any weed killer you purchase should be labeled with its chemical name, the specific weeds it will kill, and the grasses to which it can be applied.

There are a number of ways to apply herbicides. Hose-end applicators, hand sprayers, pressure spray tanks, and watering cans can all be used. Choose the method that allows the most direct and site-specific application.

Avoid spraying on windy days and remember that once a container has been filled with a herbicide, it should not be used for any purpose other than weed eradication. Do not use herbicides on a new lawn until it has grown enough to require two mowings.

Caution: If you have children or pets that play frequently on the lawn, be sure to check how long the poisons remain active.

Lawn Pests

Lawn-damaging pests fall into two categories: those that feed on leaf blades and other above-ground lawn parts and those that feed on roots and other below-ground parts.

Insects

It's important to identify which insects can damage your grass because dozens of harmless insects also inhabit your lawn. And different pests require different chemical treatments and application methods. For detailed information on how to identify and control some of the most common insects, see page 74.

Above-ground insects. Infestations of above-ground feeders are easy to spot if you look closely in the lawn itself. Cutworms, sod webworms (lawn moth larvae), leafhoppers, dichondra flea beetles, and chinch bugs are common above-ground feeders.

Below-ground insects. These insects, which include billbugs and white grubs, feed on grass roots and can devastate large sections of a lawn in a short time.

Gophers & Moles

These creatures can be a source of great frustration to gardeners, wreaking havoc on lawns and escaping all but the most persistent efforts to eradicate them.

Gophers. Serious pests in many areas, gophers resemble little bulldozers, digging a network of tunnels below the surface of lawns. Gophers eat roots, bulbs, and sometimes entire plants by pulling them down into their burrows.

Often, the first sign of gopher trouble is a fan-shaped mound of fresh, finely pulverized earth in a lawn. You may find a hole in this mound or (more often) a plug of earth blocking the exit.

Trapping is the most efficient method of catching gophers. Avoid the temptation of placing a single trap down a hole. Your chances of catching a gopher are much greater when you dig down to the main horizontal runway connecting with the surface hole and place two traps in the runway, one on either side of your excavation.

Once the traps are in place, plug the hole with fresh grass or other tender greens. Place a board or soil over the greens to block all light. Check the traps

often and clear the tunnels if the gopher has pushed soil into the traps. Be persistent: a wily gopher may avoid your first attempts.

Moles. Notorious pests in good soils, moles are primarily insectivorous, eating earthworms, bugs, and larvae, and only occasionally nibbling on greens and roots. Irrigation and rain keep them near the soil surface where they do the most damage as they tunnel, disfiguring lawns, heaving plants from the ground, and severing tender roots.

A mole's main runways, which are used repeatedly, are usually from 6 to 10 inches underground and are frequently punctuated with volcano-shaped mounds of excavated soil. Shallower burrows, created while feeding, are used for short periods and then abandoned.

Trapping is the most efficient control. The spear- or harpoon-type trap is the easiest to set because you simply position the trap above the soil. A clever mole will spring, heave out, or go around a faultily set trap.

Fungus Diseases

Threadlike lawn fungi are parasites that live off grass plants and can turn your lawn yellow or brown in a hurry. Usually, they're detected after most other pests have been eliminated and the lawn has been watered and fed with nitrogen.

Although fungus diseases rarely show all the classic symptoms, the disease information beginning on page 76 will help you identify and control any fungi that attack your yard.

Fungus problems are easier to prevent than to cure. Since fungi cannot develop in the absence of moisture, proper irrigation is the key. Water deeply; then allow the top 2 inches of soil to dry out before watering again. This eliminates the breeding grounds for fungi.

If It's Not Weeds, Pests, or Disease

Sometimes, problems linger in your lawn even after you've systematically eliminated weeds, pests, or disease as a probable cause. Here are some typical problems and their solutions.

■ *Spots on your lawn.* If spots suddenly appear on your lawn, check to see if they bear any relationship to the course you traveled with your chemical dispenser (whether a pesticide, weed killer, or fertilizer). Water the areas heavily to leach the chemicals out; the lawn will eventually recover.

If the spots persist, sight across them to see if they lie low or high in the lawn. If so, they may be getting too much or too little water. Level off a high area with a spade or fill in a low spot. Then reseed.

■ *Excessive puddling or runoff.* Soil compaction not only causes pooling

and quick runoff but also retards root growth. Too much thatch can also keep water from penetrating the soil. A proper maintenance schedule that includes dethatching and aeration (see page 65) may solve the problem.

■ *Persistent yellowing.* Lack of water or sunlight can turn a lawn yellow. Make sure enough water is getting to the area. Trees can both shade a lawn and rob it of nutrients and water. Solutions include thinning the tree to allow more sunlight to reach the lawn and adding extra fertilizer and water on lawn areas that must compete with trees.

■ *Dead spots ringed by healthy grass.* Female dogs are often responsible for stubborn dead spots in an otherwise healthy lawn. Keep the dog off the grass and soak the spots with water. If the spots persist, you'll have to reseed.

Lawn Weeds, Pests & Diseases

Despite your best intentions, some weeds, pests, or diseases will inevitably invade your lawn from time to time. Cultural controls, such as weeding or deep watering, can often eliminate the nuisance. Only if the infestation is extensive should you apply the appropriate chemical control. Take all necessary precautions whenever you use a chemical on your grass. Protect both yourself and your lawn by reading labels carefully and following the manufacturer's directions.

Lawn problems and their remedies are described on the following pages. Remember: The best protection against those problems is a lawn that's carefully maintained. For a year-round maintenance calendar, see page 79.

Common Lawn Weeds

The weeds described below, commonly found in lawns, can be controlled in several ways. You can control them culturally by keeping turf healthy. You can control them physically, by pulling or hoeing them. Or you can control them chemically with herbicides.

When you purchase a weed killer, be sure to read the label carefully. It should give the specific weeds it will control, the types of grasses you can apply it to, and instructions for use. Follow the manufacturer's directions exactly.

BERMUDA GRASS
Cynodon dactylon

■ *Description:* Bermuda grass is a perennial that thrives in warm climates. Although it's a common turf grass, it can also be a persistent weed where it grows unwanted. It spreads underground by rhizomes and above ground by seeds and stolons. Its fine leaves are pointed at the end. It's sometimes mistaken for crabgrass, but its leaves are much finer and smaller.

■ *Controls:* Cultural controls include hand-weeding, the most effective method of eradication on smaller lawns. Be sure to remove the entire underground stem; otherwise, it can start new shoots.

On larger lawns, spray isolated patches with fluazifop-butyl, sethoxydim, or glyphosate; then reseed. Repeat applications may be necessary.

ANNUAL BLUEGRASS
Poa annua

■ *Description:* Bright green annual bluegrass is fine textured and narrow leaved. It produces small, wheatlike seed blossoms that are borne on top of the grass, giving the turf an overall white-flecked appearance. Although annual bluegrass looks great in cold weather, it turns brown when the weather gets hot.

■ *Controls:* Bluegrass will die out by itself in warm weather, but it can be a stubborn weed in spring and fall.

To discourage annual bluegrass, maintain a thick-turfed, deeply rooted lawn. Eradicate by hand or apply bensulide as a preemergence herbicide.

CHICKWEED
Stellaria media

■ *Description:* Chickweed, an annual, has leaves that are smaller than postage stamps. They grow in opposite pairs on many-branched stems. This weed thrives in sheltered areas.

■ *Controls:* Keeping turf well drained helps prevent chickweed from growing. Dicamba is effective when applied in spring or fall.

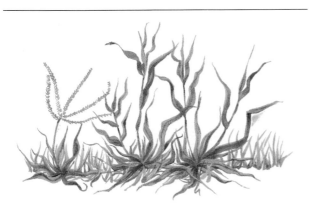

CRABGRASS
Digitaria species

■ *Description:* This is a tough annual summer weed that spreads quickly through abundant seeding. It thrives in lawns that get frequent surface watering, in underfed lawns, and in poorly drained fields.

Hairy crabgrass germinates in spring, sending up small seedlings with two to four leaves that form large, flat, stem-rooting clumps in summer. The undersides of the pale green blades are covered with coarse, tiny hairs. Fingerlike flower spikelets rise from narrow stems.

Smooth crabgrass is similar to hairy crabgrass, except that its leaves and leaf sheaths are smoother, longer, and narrower. Although not as gruesome in appearance as its hairy cousin, smooth crabgrass can infest a lawn with equal speed. Immediate eradication is necessary.

■ *Controls:* Cultural controls include keeping lawns well fertilized and vigorous to provide tough competition for weeds. To dry out crabgrass roots, water lawns deeply but not frequently.

In late winter or early spring before seedlings appear, apply a preemergent, such as DCPA (Dacthal), with a fertilizer spreader.

DALLIS GRASS
Paspalum dilatatum

■ *Description:* This perennial is a common weed during summer, its active growth period. Large, flat stalks grow in crown-shaped rings 4 to 8 inches across. The rhizomes are very closely jointed, and the seed heads are sparsely branched on long stems.

■ *Controls:* Hand-weeding is effective, but reseeding is necessary. Since dallis grass thrives in wet areas, draining or building up the lawn may be necessary.

DANDELION
Taraxacum officinale

■ *Description:* Dandelion's bright yellow flowers and stemless basal leaves are unmistakable. The weed grows from a single brownish taproot that often breaks—and can regrow—when you try to pull the plant out. It spreads by dispersing wind-borne seeds and by sprouting root crowns.

Flowering begins in spring and can often continue until frost; in mild weather, seeds can germinate year-round. The flower becomes a round, white seed head at maturity.

■ *Controls:* Proper turf maintenance procedures usually keep dandelions to a minimum. Pull out young plants before the taproot has a chance to grow deeply in the soil.

Apply MCPP in spring and fall. Spray isolated plants with glyphosate or another herbicide for broad-leaved weeds and reseed.

CURLY DOCK
Rumex crispus

■ *Description:* This broad-leaved perennial has long, narrow, dark green leaves with smooth, wavy edges. If not pulled, it sends up a tall, narrow spike of greenish flowers from the center of the plant.

■ *Controls:* Dock infestations are easy to identify and can be eradicated by hand-pulling or with the help of a small spade. For heavy infestations, use 2,4-D or dicamba in spring or fall.

KNOTWEED
Polygonum aviculare

■ *Description:* This annual, broad-leaved weed is usually light green, with small leaves growing sparsely on long,

trailing stems. However, the plants often grow close together, giving the appearance of thick foliage.

■ *Controls:* Knotweed infestations can be prevented by good maintenance practices, including dethatching and aeration. The favored chemical control is dicamba.

MALLOW, OR CHEESEWEED
Malva species

■ *Description:* This tough, low-flowering annual or biennial weed has rounded, fan-shaped green leaves at the top of a whitish stalk. There's a red spot at the base of each leaf. Mallow has a 6- to 8-month growing season, beginning in early spring.

Since the leaves stand an inch or two above the turf, the weed is easy to identify. Uncontrolled plants grow larger.

■ *Controls:* Hand-weeding is effective. Chemical controls include MCPP and dicamba.

OXALIS
Oxalis corniculata

■ *Description:* This aggressive, cloverlike weed spreads from a single taproot, which soon develops into a shallow, spreading root system. Plants may have green or reddish purple leaves and tiny, bright yellow flowers. Long, narrow, beaklike seed capsules explode like popcorn when ripe, shooting seeds as far as 6 feet.

■ *Controls:* A vigorous, well-fertilized lawn provides tough competition for oxalis. Once infestations occur, dig out small plants, tracing any runners back to the main plant. Or carefully spot-treat isolated plants with glyphosate and reseed. Triclopyr is the most effective preemergence herbicide. When weeds are gone, oryzalin is an effective preemergent.

QUACK GRASS
Agropyron repens

■ *Description:* This ungainly-looking, narrow-leaved perennial grass spreads aggressively by means of underground rhizomes. If left unmowed, it can grow from 1 to 3 feet tall. Narrow flower spikes rising from the plant resemble slender heads of wheat or rye.

■ *Controls:* Spot-treat with glyphosate and reseed.

PLANTAIN
Plantago species

■ *Description:* This cool-season perennial weed grows in a rosette shape.

Broad-leaved plantain has broad, oval-shaped leaves 3 to 6 inches long. The flower stalk is long and slender and curls slightly at the top.

Buckhorn plantain plants have long, thin leaves and a conspicuously long (up to 12 inches) stalk with a ball-like blossom cluster at the end.

■ *Controls:* Hand-pull, or apply MCPP in spring or fall before flowers form.

SPOTTED SPURGE
Euphorbia maculata

■ *Description:* This annual grows close to the ground in a thick, fast-spreading mat from a single taproot. Its small leaves are green with a red spot on the upper center. Cut stems exude a milky juice.

Spotted spurge grows aggressively in summer in almost all climates. Plants turn red orange and decline in fall as temperatures drop.

■ *Controls:* Control is difficult. Proper lawn maintenance will keep this weed to a minimum. Hoe out isolated plants early before they produce seed, or spray them with glyphosate and reseed. On lawns, use a preemergence herbicide such as DCPA (Dacthal).

Common Lawn Pests

Several different kinds of creatures can damage your lawn, some above the ground and others below ground. Different climates foster different problems: a worst offender in one region may be unknown in another.

A totally pest-free garden is neither possible nor desirable. Good maintenance procedures can go a long way toward reducing the threat of an insect infestation. Even releasing or encouraging beneficial insects can help. When you need to use insecticides, follow label directions exactly. Before you purchase a product, make sure you've correctly identified the problem. For help, contact a professional or your County Cooperative Extension office.

BILLBUGS
Sphenophorus species

■ *Description:* Billbugs are brownish black weevils with long snouts (hence, the name billbugs). The larvae are white and legless, measuring about ⅜ inch long when fully grown. They feed on roots and crowns.

■ *Susceptible plants:* All grasses, especially Bermuda grass. Old lawns in warm inland areas are most susceptible.

■ *Damage and detection.* Like white grubs, billbug larvae can destroy entire root systems if left unchecked. However, since they're active at shallower depths, the lawn cannot be rolled back, as it can after a white grub infestation, but pieces of turf can easily be picked up. To check for billbug infestations, examine the soil around browned grass roots and dig in the edges near green, healthy grass. If more than one grub per square foot is found, treat the lawn.

■ *Controls:* Diazinon and carbaryl (Sevin). Apply liquid formulations to moist turf, granular formulations to dry turf. Immediately after application, water well.

CHINCH BUGS
Blissus species

■ *Description:* Adults are dark gray to black insects that grow to less than ¼ inch long. When not in flight, the chinch bug's white wings fold flat over the body. Nymphs (immature insects) are red.

Chinch bugs crawl along grass blades and suck out the juices, leaving the lawn bleached and withered. The bugs thrive in hot weather.

■ *Susceptible plants:* St. Augustine and zoysia grasses are especially vulnerable to chinch bug infestations. Kentucky bluegrass and creeping bent grass are occasionally damaged.

■ *Damage and detection:* During infestations, yellowish patches appear in lawns, with the grass eventually dying. Sunny areas or portions under drought stress are particularly susceptible. The bugs can be found just at the edge of the damaged areas.

Check for chinch bugs by pushing a bottomless can into the soil just where the grass is beginning to turn brown. Fill the can with water. If the lawn is infested, the chinch bugs will float to the surface.

■ *Controls:* Diazinon and chlorpyrifos (Dursban). Mow and water before treatment; apply late in the day to moist turf. Do not water or mow for 24 hours.

CUTWORMS
Psudaletia species

■ *Description:* These thick-skinned, dark, 1- to 2-inch-long larvae often have spots or longitudinal stripes. When disturbed, they curl up, feigning death. At maturity, cutworms become nocturnal, brownish gray moths with a wingspan from 1 to 1½ inches.

■ *Susceptible plants:* All grasses and dichondra.

■ *Damage and detection:* The larvae feed off grass leaves and crowns, leaving small, brown, irregular patches in the grass. During the day, they hide in the thatch layer.

To detect cutworms, mix 1 tablespoon household detergent in 1 gallon water and pour evenly over a square yard of lawn area. Larvae will come to the surface. Treat when five or more larvae are found per square yard.

■ *Controls:* Thatch removal effectively eliminates the cutworms' hiding place. Chemical controls include acephate (Orthene), chlorpyrifos (Dursban), and diazinon. Mow and water before treatment; apply late in the day to moist turf. Do not water or mow for 24 hours.

FLEA BEETLES
Chaetocnema repens

■ *Description:* Adult flea beetles are black and very tiny and look somewhat like small fleas; they'll jump a foot or two into the air when disturbed. The larvae live in the soil and are rarely seen.

■ *Susceptible plants:* Dichondra.

■ *Damage and detection:* Although miniscule, these innocent-looking pests can devastate a dichondra lawn in a relatively short time. Adult flea beetles feed on the leaf's surface and remove the soft tissue. The remaining plant skeleton will twist and turn brown as though suffering from fertilizer burn or lack of water.

Upon close examination, you can spot the tiny beetles sitting on the plant leaves. When disturbed, the area will suddenly come alive with tiny, jumping insects.

■ *Controls:* Diazinon and chlorpyrifos (Dursban). Mow and water before treatment; apply late in the day to moist turf. Do not water or mow for 24 hours.

LEAFHOPPERS
Cicadellidae family

■ *Description:* Like tiny (⅛- to ¼-inch) grasshoppers, these pale green, gray, or yellow insects are very active. When disturbed, they may fly or hop short distances. Immature leafhoppers are the same colors as adults but lack wings.

■ *Susceptible plants:* All grasses. Dichondra is not usually attacked.

■ *Damage and detection:* Leafhoppers are easy to detect since they fly up in swarms as you walk through the lawn. They suck juices from the leaves and, if unchecked, can leave the lawn pale and dry.

■ *Controls:* Diazinon and carbaryl (Sevin). Mow and water before treatment; apply late in the day to moist turf. Do not water or mow for 24 hours.

SOD WEBWORMS (LAWN MOTHS)
Crambus sperryellus

■ *Description:* Sod webworms, slender gray caterpillars with black spots, are larvae of whitish or buff-colored moths that have a 1-inch wingspan. The webworms get their name from the silken tunnels they spin in thatch layers.

A silvery white stripe is easy to spot on the lawn moth's forewing. The moths hide in the grass during the day and fly in a zigzag pattern when disturbed. They usually fly at night, dropping their eggs while in flight. The larvae hatch and begin feeding on turf blades and stems.

■ *Susceptible plants:* All grasses. Especially vulnerable are bent grasses, bluegrasses, and all new lawns.

■ *Damage and detection:* Patchy brown areas on the lawn, often with pencil-size holes made by birds digging for the webworms, indicate an infestation. To detect webworms, bring them to the surface by mixing 1 tablespoon household detergent in 1 gallon water and pouring evenly over a 1-square-yard area. Treat when 15 or more webworms are found per square yard.

■ *Controls:* Proper lawn maintenance, including watering, aeration, and dethatching, will reduce the infestation. If necessary, treat with diazinon or chlorpyrifos (Dursban). Mow and water before treatment; apply late in the day to moist turf. Do not water or mow for 24 hours.

WHITE GRUBS
Cyclocephala species

■ *Description:* The larvae are large (from 1 to 1½ inches long) and C-shaped when at rest. Their most distinguishing feature is three pairs of legs. The adults are brown with reddish heads and are known as May beetles or June bugs (it's during those months that they emerge from the ground as adults). Japanese beetles also emerge in spring.

■ *Susceptible plants:* All grasses.

■ *Damage and detection:* White grubs feed beneath the surface, destroying grass roots. In areas where infestation is heavy, the roots are completely eaten away and the lawn can be rolled back like sod. Once the symptoms appear in late summer, most of the damage has been done.

To check for white grubs, dig up the soil under brown spots in mid-July. If more than one grub per square foot is found, treat the entire lawn by early August.

■ *Controls:* Diazinon and chlorpyrifos (Dursban). Apply liquid formulations to moist turf, granular to dry turf; then water well. Chemicals work best when there's little thatch.

Common Lawn Diseases

Most lawn diseases are the result of various fungi. But sometimes, unfavorable environmental conditions or poor maintenance practices can cause disease. The buildup of thatch creates favorable conditions for the development of fungal diseases, as do too much or too little fertilizer (or fertilizer applied at the wrong time of year) and poorly drained soil that stays moist for long periods of time.

Proper maintenance procedures are explained in this chapter. When disease persists, you may have to resort to a fungicide. As with any chemical, read the label carefully and follow directions to the letter.

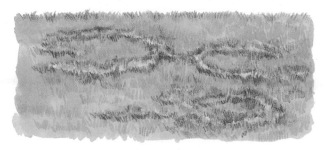

BROWN PATCH
Rhizoctonia solani

■ *Symptoms:* Brown patch is characterized by small, irregularly shaped brown spots that may enlarge as the disease strengthens. The centers of the spots may recover, exposing large brown circles (like smoke rings) in the lawn. The grass blades become water soaked, turn yellowish brown, and die.

■ *Susceptible grasses:* Bent grasses, Bermuda grasses, bluegrasses, fescues, ryegrasses, and St. Augustine grass.

■ *Controls:* Minimize shade and aerate the lawn. Irrigate 6 inches deep as needed. Avoid fertilizers high in nitrogen. Fungicidal controls include benomyl, chlorothalonil, and thiophanate.

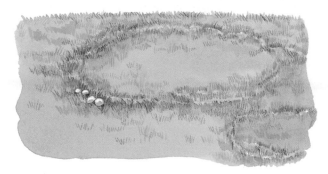

FAIRY RING
Marasmius oreades

■ *Symptoms:* Fairy ring appears as small, circular patches of dark green grass, often followed by dead grass. Mushrooms may or may not be present.

■ *Susceptible grasses:* All grasses.

■ *Controls:* Aerate the lawn, apply a fertilizer high in nitrogen, and keep the lawn wet for 3 to 5 days. There is no effective fungicidal control.

DOLLAR SPOT
Sclerotinia homeocarpa

■ *Symptoms:* Dollar spot attacks lawns in numerous small (about the size of a silver dollar) bleached or gray spots. When the fungus first starts, the infected areas have a water-soaked appearance. Sometimes, spots merge to make large, straw-colored areas.

■ *Susceptible grasses:* Bent grasses, Bermuda grasses, bluegrasses, fescues, and ryegrasses.

■ *Controls:* Dethatch the lawn and irrigate 6 inches deep as needed. Apply a fertilizer high in nitrogen. Fungicidal controls include anilazine, benomyl, and thiophanate.

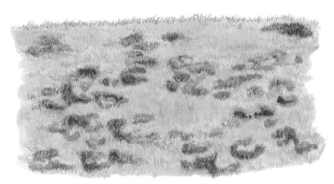

FUSARIUM PATCH
Fusarium nivale

■ *Symptoms:* Common in the central states and the Northeast, fusarium patch shows up as tan or brown spots 2 to 12 inches in diameter. Look for weblike threads in thatch or on dew-covered grass.

■ *Susceptible grasses:* Bent grasses, bluegrasses, fescues, and ryegrasses.

■ *Controls:* Minimize shade, aerate the lawn, and improve drainage. Avoid fertilizers high in nitrogen. Fungicidal controls include benomyl and thiophanate. Apply fungicide early in the fall.

GREASE SPOT
Pythium

■ *Symptoms:* Infected blades turn dark and become matted together, giving a greasy appearance in streaks through the lawn. Sometimes, a white, cottony mold appears on leaf blades.

■ *Susceptible grasses:* All grasses, particularly new lawns.

■ *Controls:* Minimize shade and aerate the lawn. Apply water early in the day and avoid excess watering. Control with metalaxyl.

RUST
Puccinia

■ *Symptoms:* Small reddish pustules form in circular or elongated groups on older leaf blades and stems; the blades eventually shrivel and die. Rub a white cloth over a suspected infection: if the cloth picks up an orange color, it's rust disease.

■ *Susceptible grasses:* Bluegrasses and ryegrasses.

■ *Controls:* Apply a fertilizer high in nitrogen and water regularly. Triadimefon is the most effective fungicide. Anilazine and mancozeb are also helpful.

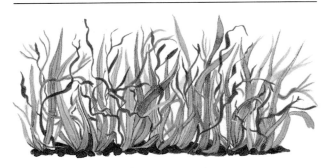

RED THREAD
Coricium fuciforme

■ *Symptoms:* Small patches of dead grass appear, followed by spiderlike webs of bright pink threads that bind blades together. The lawn yellows in patches 2 to 12 inches in diameter. This fungus likes cool, moist weather.

■ *Susceptible grasses:* Bent grasses, bluegrasses, fescues, and ryegrasses.

■ *Controls:* Apply a high-nitrogen fertilizer in late fall. Minimize shade on the lawn. Fungicidal controls include chlorothalonil and mancozeb.

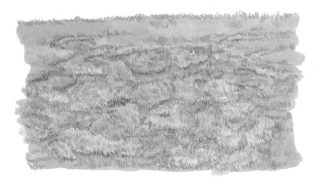

SNOW MOLD
Typhula

■ *Symptoms:* As snow melts, snow mold appears as dirty white patches in the lawn. The margins between these patches are rather distinct, and the dead grass pulls up easily.

■ *Susceptible grasses:* Bent grasses, bluegrasses, and fescues.

■ *Controls:* Aerate the lawn and improve drainage, if possible. Try to reduce snow pileup. Fungicidal controls include benomyl and thiophanate (apply before the first snowfall).

Lawn Maintenance Calendar

	Cool-season Grasses	Warm-season Grasses
Spring 	**Seed** after ground warms. Lay sod anytime. **Mow** weekly. Towards end of season, raise cutting height to 2 inches. **Water** more as growth increases. **Fertilize** when temperature reaches 60°F and again about a month later. If lush growth doesn't result, add iron in West; adjust pH with lime in East. **Dethatch and aerate,** if needed, early in season. **Control weeds** with a preemergence herbicide, if necessary.	**Seed** or sprig after danger of frost has passed. Plant plugs before warming begins. Lay sod anytime. **Mow** more often as growth increases. **Water** more as growth increases. **Fertilize** early in season and again about a month later. If lush growth doesn't result, add iron in West; adjust pH with lime in East. **Dethatch and aerate,** if needed, late in season. **Control weeds** with a preemergence herbicide, if necessary.
Summer 	**Lay sod** anytime. Reseed late in summer. If seeding in fall, prepare soil. **Mow** regularly as temperatures rise, increasing cutting height to reduce weeds and improve drought and heat tolerance. **Water** slowly, deeply, and infrequently to discourage weeds and keep grass healthy. **Fertilize** no later than early June, if at all. **Aerate,** if needed, to improve water penetration. **Control weeds** and disease with regular mowing and deep, infrequent watering.	**Seed** early in season. Lay sod anytime. **Mow** regularly as temperatures rise, increasing cutting height. Leave grass clippings on lawn. **Water** slowly, deeply, and infrequently to discourage weeds and keep grass healthy. **Fertilize,** if necessary. **Aerate,** if needed, to improve water penetration. **Control weeds** and disease with regular mowing and deep, infrequent watering.
Fall 	**Seed** while soil is still warm. Lay sod anytime. **Mow** often if lawn is vigorous. **Water** less often unless lawn is new. **Fertilize** several times, about a month apart. **Dethatch,** if needed, early in fall; then fertilize. Aerate, if needed, to improve water penetration. **Control weeds,** if necessary, with a preemergence herbicide that prevents germination of winter weeds.	**Seed** only in very early fall. In mid-season, overseed with annual or perennial ryegrass or fescues for green winter lawns. Lay sod anytime. **Mow** as needed. **Water** less often. **Fertilize** early in season for a green lawn later in fall and earlier in spring. **Control weeds,** if necessary, with a preemergence herbicide that prevents germination of winter weeds.
Winter 	**Lay sod** in mild-winter areas. **Mow** as needed. **Water** as needed. **Fertilize,** if necessary, only in mildest winter climates. **Aerate,** if needed, to improve water penetration, but do not dethatch. **Control weeds** with a preemergence herbicide, if necessary. If snow mold damaged lawn last year, treat it now.	**Lay sod** anytime. **Mow** weekly if lawn is overseeded with annual ryegrass; otherwise, mow as needed. **Water** when needed. **Fertilize** in late winter if lawn stays green. **Aerate,** if needed, to improve water penetration. **Control weeds** with a preemergence herbicide, if necessary.

Index